DENIZENS OF
ALIEN WORLDS

A Study of Education, Inequality
and Polarization in Pakistan

DENIZENS OF ALIEN WORLDS

A Study of Education, Inequality and Polarization in Pakistan

Tariq Rahman

OXFORD
UNIVERSITY PRESS

OXFORD
UNIVERSITY PRESS

Great Clarendon Street, Oxford ox2 6DP

Oxford University Press is a department of the University of Oxford.
It furthers the University's objective of excellence in research, scholarship,
and education by publishing worldwide in

Oxford New York

Auckland Bangkok Buenos Aires Cape Town Chennai
Dar es Salaam Delhi Hong Kong Istanbul Karachi Kolkata
Kuala Lumpur Madrid Melbourne Mexico City Mumbai Nairobi
São Paulo Shanghai Taipei Tokyo Toronto

Oxford is a registered trade mark of Oxford University Press
in the UK and in certain other countries

ISBN 0 19 597863 3

Typeset in Times
Printed in Pakistan by
Kagzi Printers, Karachi.
Published by
Ameena Saiyid, Oxford University Press
Plot No. 38, Sector 15, Korangi Industrial Area, PO Box 8214
Karachi-74900, Pakistan.

For
Hana, Tania and Fahad

Whatever (harm) a foe may do to a foe, or a hater to a hater, an
ill-directed mind can do one far greater (harm).
(Dhammapada)

CONTENTS

LIST OF ABBREVIATIONS

Less used abbreviations are given in the text where they occur. This is a list of abbreviations which are spread out at several places in the text.

A' Level	Advanced Level School Leaving Certificate of British Boards of Education
D	*Dawn* [English daily]
J	*Jang* [Urdu daily]
LAD-WP	*Legislative Assembly Debates-West Pakistan* [Used for legislative assemblies no matter what they were called
M	*The Muslim* [English daily]
MLR	Martial Law Regulation
MN	*Morning News* [English daily]
N	*The Nation* [English daily]
NGOs	Non Government Organizations
NW	*Nawai Waqt* [Urdu daily]
O' Level	Ordinary Level School Leaving Certificate of British Boards of Education.
PT	*Pakistan Times* [English daily]
WAPDA	Water and Power Development Authority

GLOSSARY

Jihad	Religious war for the sake of Islam. The Muslim concept of *bellum justum* (just war). Also used for any struggle for righteousness.
Madrassa	Religious seminary.
Maktab	Religious school for small children. Also used for all schools before the arrival of the British.
Maulvi	Muslim religious figure who leads prayers and performs the functions of a priest.
Munshi	Clerk, accountant.
Raj	Rule.
Shaheed	Martyr.
Ulema	Islamic religious scholars.

PREFACE

The idea for this brief study came to mind when Professor Craig Baxter, Professor Emeritus of Politics and History at Juniata College, USA, asked me to contribute a chapter on education for his forthcoming book on Pakistan. I had already been working on aspects of education in three earlier books published by the Oxford University Press: *Language and Politics in Pakistan* (1996); *Language, Education and Culture* (1999); and *Language, Ideology and Power: Language-Learning Among the Muslims of Pakistan and North India* (2002). I therefore, thought it would be easy to write the asked for chapter. However, much to my chagrin, I discovered that this was not going to be an easy task. What I had written was outdated, purely historical, or had been written from the point of view of language policy. I simply could not confine myself to a cut and paste job.

I then made my usual forays in the field, went to the libraries and put together a chapter that as per the requirement, was quite brief. Then something unusual happened. Dr Kaiser Bengali, Acting Managing Director of the Social Policy and Development Centre (SPDC) in Karachi, asked me to contribute a report on the system of schooling in Pakistan, adding that he would pay me for this research—something that has happened only once before in my research experience. The sum he offered as consultancy fees seemed somewhat extravagant, but he reassured me that, in his opinion, I had never been rewarded adequately for my labour before. This was because I did not know how to get the 'rewards', which is why I had not entered the consultancy business. I told him that money, specially large sums, made me apprehensive about how much freedom I could exercise. He assured me that I would be free to publish my work—warts and all—whenever and wherever I wanted, provided I made it clear that the survey and money for this research came from the SPDC. I agreed to these terms and began my research.

I hired two research assistants, Shahid Gondal and Imran, who had three months, December 2002 and January–February 2003, to take questionnaires (for survey 2003) to schools and madrassas. I went

myself to the elitist English-medium schools and other institutions of
Rawalpindi, Lahore, Karachi and Peshawar.

Shahid Gondal went to Mandi Bahauddin (his hometown), and
Imran went to Multan, Faisalabad and Lahore. I thank both Shahid
and Imran without whose efforts this survey would not have been
completed. I thank the SPDC for having paid for both of them and
making life comfortable for me. I had written all my previous books
unsupported by any institution, and had to undergo great personal
expense for the research. This time it was different, and now I know
how consultants do research.

The school survey, except for the section on cadet colleges/public
schools, was over by February 2003. At this time, I was appointed
Professor and Director of the Chair on Quaid-i-Azam and Freedom
Movement. Here I had funds for research as well as the services of a
dedicated researcher, Rao Iqbal, who is Research Fellow on the Chair.
Therefore, I decided to do some more research on the universities and
the cadet colleges. Rao Iqbal went to Bahawalpur, Faisalabad, Lahore
and Hassanabdal, and I went to Murree to collect data and to administer
questionnaires to students and faculty. The Chair paid for this part of
the research, and I am delighted that somebody had the wisdom of
establishing a chair for research on Pakistan.

My thanks to Mr Rao Iqbal are difficult to express. He was highly
dedicated to the whole project from the beginning to the end. He also
helped with the proof reading. He is an asset to the Quaid-i-Azam
Chair and I am sure he will continue his efforts to produce quality
research.

This book has some weaknesses and some strengths. The
weaknesses are that passages on the history of schools, madrassas and
universities, which are based on my previous research as published in
Language and Politics in Pakistan (1996), *Language, Education and
Culture* (1999) and *Language, Ideology and Power* (2002) have been
included here. Nevertheless, this was necessary to understand the
historical background of education in Pakistan.

The strengths are that all the data pertaining to education in my
books and articles has now been put together in one place. Moreover,
and this is really worth noting, new data has been obtained on all the
educational institutions. Some of this data is really remarkable because
it has never been published before. The significance of this data is that
we now have an empirical base for making the assertion that elitist
education gets funded whereas the masses are starved of funds. I have

also consulted other sources, both secondary and primary, and met teachers and students in many parts of the country from the end of 2002 to the summer of 2003. These meetings have given me valuable insight and make the book worthwhile. The research has made available a new survey of students and teachers of schools, madrassas, colleges, private universities and public universities. The socio-economic class of these respondents has been determined and questions on sensitive issues have been asked through questionnaires in Urdu and English. This is new data that should be of interest for those who want to understand how Pakistani society is divided according to class, and how polarized the different classes are.

As expected, some persons approached refused to cooperate, refused to give data and did not even agree to complete questionnaires or get them completed by others. Such people and institutions make research much more difficult. However, let me end by thanking those countless others—teachers, students, administrators—who helped me and made this book possible. In the end I take this opportunity to thank Ameena Saiyid, Managing Director of the Oxford University Press (Pakistan) who encouraged me to submit this book to OUP.

TARIQ RAHMAN
Ph.D.
National Distinguished Professor
Quaid-i-Azam University
Islamabad

1

INTRODUCTION

There are a number of books and official reports on education. Indeed, as Pakistanis look at the increasing violence and inequality in their society, they blame the education system. Almost all problems—increasing population, corruption, political instability, technological backwardness, feudalism, the increasing power of the coercive apparatus of the state, lack of human rights—are blamed on lack of education. Ironically, both those who believe in democracy and those who do not, justify their analysis of society with reference to education. Those who believe in 'benevolent' dictatorship (no matter what they call it) argue that in a country with so much illiteracy and such poor standards of education, it is unrealistic to expect democracy to flourish. The number of people who have made this argument include former presidents Iskander Mirza and Ayub Khan and, of course, this belief is as strong now as ever. Those who argue on the other side, claim that formal education does not make people any more altruistic or dispassionate than the lack of it. Moreover, they add, if people are not educated that is the fault of their rulers. To take away the power of vote on account of this is to compound the injury.

Because education is such an all-absorbing subject one would expect it to have been well researched. Unfortunately, this is not true. There is a plethora of data; there are repetitions of policies; there is much quantitative increase in schools and teachers and so on—but there is very little analysis.

For instance, Umme Salma Zaman's *Banners Unfurled* (1981), which is billed as a 'critical analysis' of education, contains chapters on such contentious issues as politics, the bureaucracy, language and Ayub Khan's regime. However, though the book has some critical remarks about specific matters, it fails to give an overall analysis in terms of explanatory analytical concepts such as power, class, and ideology. But Zaman's book is among the better studies on education in the country. Most other books tend to take a moralistic line that aims at defending government policies while talking vaguely about what 'should be' rather than 'what is' and, more importantly, why is it the way it is? For instance, Syed Abdul Quddus describes all aspects of the educational system of Pakistan but his analysis of ethnicity is essentially moralistic and refers to conspiracy theories for support. For instance, in the chapter on national integration he says:

> It is high time that we should educate our simple and innocent people to look through the dirty game of the vested interests and the unscrupulous politicians. These who refuse to believe the existence of provincialism, parochialism and regionalism are living in fools' paradise and playing the proverbial ostrich; for the provincialism is a multi-headed monster [sic] (Quddus, S.A. 1979: 261).

For a book published in 1979, eight years after Bangladesh seceded from Pakistan as a result of a nationalist movement in response to the denial of a rightful share in goods, services and power in the state, to call ethnicity merely 'provincialism' reveals the theoretical lack of sophistication of the analysis. By this time there were many books on ethnicity—after all, Nathan Glazer and Daniel P. Moynihan had published their seminal work *Beyond the Melting Pot* (1963) sixteen years earlier. They had claimed that, among other things, modernity creates or reinforces ethnic identity. This meant that language-based assertions of identity, which Quddus was alluding to, were not hangovers from the past to be dismissed as 'provincialism'. They were realities which the educational system affected one way or the other.

Aftab A. Kazi, from Sindh wrote a book on ethnicity called *Ethnicity and Education in Nation-Building in Pakistan* (1994). This was written at a time when most educated Sindhis were acutely aware of their Sindhi ethnic identity and the name of Feroze Ahmed, who had written much on this subject, was a legend in Sindh (see Ahmed 1998). The author has, indeed, taken some major theories of ethnicity into account and has given a good analysis of Pakistan's educational history in relation to ethnicity. He has also pointed out that the ruling elite has overemphasized Islamic ideology and used Urdu to counteract ethnic tendencies. In his zeal to correct the centrist tendencies of right wing writers on education, Kazi overemphasizes the Sindhi nationalist viewpoint at times. On the whole, however, this book is theoretically more sophisticated than most other books on education.

The book by Naseem Jaffer Quddus is as moralistic in tone as most right wing, nationalist studies tend to be. He, too, tells us that if 'Pakistan is to survive as a nation, it is absolutely essential to evolve a common national language' (Quddus, N.J. 1990: 216). He also complains that 'our educators do not work with missionary spirit' (ibid., 359) without giving a scientific explanation of why they should do so? And, if they do not, why is it that they do not. In short, there is no theoretical analysis nor reference to empirical evidence for the pronouncements in the book.

The Crisis of Education in Pakistan (Hayes 1987) provides relevant information about the number of institutions, major policies and the structure of educational administration. However, there is no in-depth understanding of the deeper problems of which the low educational standards are a symptom. However, in many ways this is a fairly good introductory work on education. It is useful because there are hardly any other comparable introductory works with some attempt at providing empirical evidence. For instance, Mukhtar Ahmed Bhatti's work on secondary education (1982), is full of facts and data but is, for that very reason, only as useful as one of the many reports and fact sheets on the subject available in the country. However, it does have a lot of data on school education up to 1986.

As the 1980s were dominated by General Ziaul Haq with his emphasis on Islamization, there are a large number of essays, pamphlets and articles both in English and Urdu on rendering education 'Islamic'. This often meant emphasizing Arabic, including Quranic verses in the textbooks for children to memorize, as well as stories from the Islamic history in every course. However, there were some attempts at presenting well-informed and theoretically sophisticated understanding of the concept of education in Islam. Some papers presented at the First World Conference on Muslim education organized by King Abdul Aziz University, Jeddah (3 March–8 April 1977) are a good example of this (al-Attas 1978). Similarly, the famous Sindhi scholar, N.A. Baloch, has presented some valuable historical insights into Muslim educational ideas in his brief book on *Education Based on Islamic Values* (2000). But these contributions, valuable from a philosophical or historical perspective, are very few and far between. Moreover, they provide no insights into the way education in

Pakistan is related to the social, economic and political realities of our country.

In general, education seems to have been a neglected subject by liberal scholars and social scientists. Sociologist Rubina Saigol's *Education: Critical Perspectives*, is a good beginning (Saigol 1993). This book comprises essays on subjects such as 'education and social class', 'education and religion', democracy, violence, and women from a liberal viewpoint. Saigol's later work deals with the manner in which educational discourse creates notions of identity which subjugate women in a male-dominated social system. These are excellent examples of sophisticated theoretical analysis, and illuminate much that was not clear before (Saigol 1995 and 2000). Saigol also refers to the way education creates classes and identities that enable one to take action. If identities are constructed on hatred, there will be violence. This, unfortunately, is what our anti-India, anti-women texts are doing (Saigol 2000: 73 and 254).

Saigol had referred to Pervez Hoodbhoy's book *Muslims and Science* (1991), which was perhaps the first attempt to challenge Ziaul Haq's regime's 'view of education as an ideological tool which should serve the interests of the religious lobby' (Saigol 1993: 1). Hoodbhoy also confronted those elements of the state and the education lobby who fill children's textbooks with anti-India and pro-war views (Hoodbhoy and Nayyar 1985). This is a struggle which goes on even today as will be brought out later in this book. Hoodbhoy also edited a book, *Education and the State* (1998), that contains essays on the economics of education, the examination system, the role of NGOs in education, madrassas, universities and so on. Most of these essays are of high quality but some lack an understanding of, or familiarity with, primary sources. Moreover, the book does not touch upon the cadet colleges or the private universities proliferating nowadays. Nor does the book look at education from the viewpoint of socio-economic class and the students' worldview, i.e. what do they think about militancy (as in Kashmir) and tolerance (of minorities).

The objectives of the present book are: to give a historical overview of the development of educational institutions in British India; to describe how schools and universities are situated in contemporary Pakistan; to understand how Pakistani society is polarized along socio-economic lines and how, at least at the school level, this results in polarization in worldview as well.

Pakistan is a poor country. Poverty is defined as the condition in which, among other things, one cannot even get the minimum caloric requirement of 2,350 calories per day. In 2000-1, one needed an income of Rs 748 per month to buy food containing these many calories. According to a survey of 726 households in February 2003, about 31.8 per cent people are below this poverty line. Even worse, this poverty is unevenly spread out with tremendous differences between the rich and the poor, the city and the village, and between men and women. For instance, the class-wise share of income in the country is as follows:

Percentage Share of Income Between Socio-economic Classes

Year	Lowest 20%	Middle 60%	Highest 20%
1998-9	6.2	44.1	49.7

Source: GoP 2003: 50

Poverty has increased since 1979 when the share of the lowest 20 per cent was 7.4 per cent, while that of the highest was 45 per cent. The ratio of the highest (22 per cent) to the lowest (20 per cent) rose from 6.1 per cent to 8 per cent (GoP 2003: 50).

The disparity between the cities and the villages too is striking. In 2003, while 38.65 per cent people are below the poverty line in the villages, those below that level in the cities are 22.39 per cent.

In short, inequalities in income—and related to that many other factors including access to quality education—are acute and, what is worse, seem to be growing. One of the major emphases of this study is to find out what differences there are in the educational institutions of the rich and the poor and to what extent the state itself creates them or, at least, perpetuates them.

For the historical part of the study I have consulted historical sources. For the contemporary, descriptive part, I have looked at the budgets of institutions, their model of governance, their fees structure and other relevant facts. Students, teachers and administrators have been interviewed and interacted with to obtain insights into their experiences. For the third part of the book, assisted by my research associates, I have carried out a survey using the non-random stratified, cluster sampling method (see Annexure 2). The clusters were the different educational institutions—elitist English-medium schools charging tuition fees of at least Rs 2,500 per month at the O level (class 10); cadet colleges/public schools; Urdu-medium (government schools; Sunni Islamic seminaries or madrassas); public universities, private universities and government colleges. Our stratas were (a) male (b) female (c) teachers (d) students.

In the schools only class-10 and equivalent were chosen, but in the universities students of professional, bachelor's as well as master's levels were approached. The respondents were given questionnaires to complete while the researcher was present. In the universities some members of the faculty did not, however, fill in the questionnaires immediately.

The survey had to be confined to the major cities. Unfortunately, Quetta and Hyderabad could not be covered. This means that we have the views of Punjabis and some urban residents of Peshawar and Karachi. The survey, then, does not represent rural and small-town Pakistan; it also does not represent the Sindhis, Balochis and the Pakhtuns adequately.

These are major drawbacks and I will make no attempt to conceal them or minimize their significance. However, as inadequate and unrepresentative as the sample certainly is, it does at least give some clues as to how the educated, mostly Punjabi, urban students and teachers—perhaps the most powerful opinion-making pressure group of the future—is thinking about issues upon which lies the future of Pakistan. Is this not worth investigating? This I leave the reader to decide. This book has eight chapters, including the introduction. Chapter 2 deals with education policies; Chapter 3, the Urdu medium schools; Chapter 4, the English-medium schools; Chapter 5, the madrassas; Chapter 6, higher education; Chapter 7, on recommendations and proposals to improve the educational system. Chapter 8 provides concluding remarks, outlining the relationship between education policies, expenditure on different kinds of educational institutions by the state and the students, and, finally the inequality produced by such a system of education. Each chapter combines a historical overview, some facts about the institutions at present and an analysis of the worldview of the students and the teachers of the institution. There is new data in the annexures, and there is a bibliography and an index.

2

EDUCATION POLICIES

The first meeting on education was held in Karachi from 27 November
to 1 December 1947. This was a time when South Asia was literally
running red with the blood of people slaughtered on both sides of the
borders of the newly independent states of Pakistan and India. Thus,
despite the collection of luminaries from the world of policy-makers
and bureaucracy assembled on that mild winter day in Karachi, the
then capital of Pakistan, education was obviously not a subject of high
priority at the time. This was a period when the existence of the nation
itself was under threat. The armed forces were inadequate and
disorganized; Kashmir was already a flashpoint; there was hardly any
money to run the new state; and to top it all there was a constant
influx of refugees crossing paths with the Hindus and Sikhs on their
outward journey. There was panic and chaos everywhere; this was
certainly not the best of times to think of education.

Nevertheless, the participants of the meeting, besides setting up the
infrastructure (Advisory Board of Education, Inter-University Board,
Council of Technical Education), set out to consider what should be
the ideological basis of education. This was the first point on the
supplementary agenda and it read as follows:

> What should be the ideological basis of education? Whether the Islamic
> conception of universal brotherhood of man, social democracy and social
> justice should constitute this ideological basis—cultivation of democratic
> virtues, i.e. tolerance, self-help, self-sacrifice, human kindliness etc and
> the consciousness of common citizenship as opposed to provincial
> exclusiveness (GoP 1947).

The question was merely rhetorical because everyone was expected to
reject the concept of 'provincial exclusiveness'. Really the 'ideological
basis' was a thinly concealed attempt to contain, oppose and eliminate
ethnic threat—albeit one which had not made itself visible yet, though

some young Bengalis had started to put forth the Bengali language as a contender for the national language of the country (Rahman 1996: 84-86).

Though Islam was to be used to oppose identity-formation on the basis of ethnicity, the Quaid-i-Azam's message made it very clear that democracy, and not theocracy was what he had in mind, 'The impression that Pakistan, being an Islamic State, is a theocratic State, is being sedulously fostered in certain quarters with the sole object of discrediting it in the eyes of the world.' This was not acceptable to him (GoP 1947: 6). He went on to equate Islam with democracy, freedom, civil rights and rights of property. However, since its inception Pakistan's ruling elite has used Islam to combat ethnicity; to foster an ideologically based identity as opposed to the Indian conception of area-based, secular identity; and to legitimize their rule. Ironically, the rulers have interpreted Islam broadly to mean democracy, the welfare state, socialism and authoritarian rule, as and when it suited them. The ethnic leaders have opposed Pakistan's rulers because, in the name of national identity, their own identity is denied. The religious leaders feel that only they can interpret Islam.

Nevertheless, whatever the interpretation of the rulers subsequently, at that time the members of the committee had to lay down the ground rules. Among the things they decided was to include Islamic studies in the curriculum; declare that the syllabi would be in conformity with Islam; and make Urdu compulsory for all. Urdu was a symbol of unity for the ruling elite. After all, they had used it during the Hindi-Urdu controversy to mobilize the Indian Muslims into a unified community to oppose the Hindus (Rahman 1996: 65-78). Now Urdu, like Islam, was perceived as useful in order to create a unified Pakistani nation consisting of Punjabis, Sindhis, Pathans, Mohajirs, Balochis and, above all, Bengalis. Moreover, this was a time when the European nation-state was the model, and all these model states, except Switzerland, had one national language. Indeed, as Benedict Anderson has pointed out, the great European print languages, along with the national flag, the museum, the census etc, had created the 'imagined communities' called nations (Anderson 1983). What the leaders did not realize was that Pakistan and India were multi-ethnic, multi-lingual and multi-cultural states, which had been carved out by their colonial masters.

However, economically speaking, it would cost less if everybody operated in one language. Indeed the costs of operations would increase astronomically if many languages were used. Thus for political, ideological, pragmatic and economic reasons, they emphasized the use of Urdu as a lingua franca. This decision sowed the seeds of the eventual separation of East Pakistan, exactly the thing the rulers had hoped to avoid.

The rulers only created policies which, according to their lights, aimed at countering ethnic and religious divisions. They did not create educational policies to counter divisions along socio-economic class divides. In fact they preferred to ignore these lines of divide altogether. Thus, in accordance with Quaid-i-Azam's message that English 'must for some considerable time to come retain its pride of place both in the sphere of our university education and as a means of international communication' (GoP 1947: 11), the committees decided to retain English as a compulsory language at school. What the report did not make explicit, however, was that besides government schools for which the policies were being made, there were other schools (convents, European type schools, public schools on the lines of Eton and Harrow, elitist armed forces schools) which used English as the medium of instruction. These would carry on their business just as they did in the days of the British. And it would be in these schools in which the elite of the new state would be educated. Thus the implication was that the new state would actually patronize and subsidize these schools, and for all the talk about Urdu, the state's real policy would be to create an unequal education system with the masses being educated in Urdu, Bengali and Sindhi (in rural and interior Sindh). All other languages were ignored though the provinces were free to teach them if they liked. Of course the elite was educated in English. This consequence of the policy, despite its divisive potential, was not mentioned at all.

In these early days religious threat had to be countered as well. The Pakistani elite did not do this by direct coercion, as was done in Turkey and Iran earlier. Indeed, the redeeming feature of Pakistan's elite has always been that it has not been as openly coercive, except on occasions in Bengal, Sindh and parts of Balochistan, as the elite has been in most non-democratic countries. So, against the religious lobby too the proposed modus operandi was co-optation. The committee suggested that 'steps should be taken to bring these madrassas into line with the existing system of general education.' (GoP 1947-22) More than half a century later, this proposal is still being bandied about with little success because the madrassas run on charity and endowments and not on government funds.

The major decisions of this first meeting on educational policy have been given in some detail in order to show that, in the final analysis, these are the operational principles of all subsequent education policies to this day. Latter day documents use different words and lay out different strategies to achieve what was outlined right in the beginning: countering the threat of ethnicity; countering religious lobbies as rivals for power; safeguarding the privileged position of the Westernized elite; and consequently, creating a citizenry which would support state policies and be trained to be employed in subordinate positions.

That this is true is borne out by looking at the educational policy documents that various governments have churned out periodically. Dr Kaiser Bengali (1999) has already carried out this exercise, and it is unnecessary to repeat it. However, it is necessary here to point out the major features of some of the more important reports.

The First Meeting of the Advisory Board of Education for Pakistan held in Karachi 7-9 June 1948 (GoP 1948) took practical measures to implement the major political and ideological policies announced earlier. At this stage it appears that the government's policy was to teach children in the mother tongue, switch after five to six years of schooling to Urdu and then teach in English at the higher levels. However, Appendix VI suggested the replacement of English by Urdu by 1957 or so. The policy was also to Islamize education. However, up to 1958, nothing concrete was done to change the status quo.

A perusal of the minutes of the meetings of the Advisory Board of Education (GoP 1949, 1950, 1954 etc.) reveals three kinds of proposals: ideological and political; pertaining to quality; pertaining to quantity. The ideological and political, as explained earlier, are real or apparent. The real ones, for instance, are to strengthen the power of the elite; the apparent ones are to develop the peoples' educational abilities. Thus, while really English and Urdu hold sway much lip service is paid to the 'regional' languages.

Policies about improving quality: achieving 80 per cent literacy in twenty years (GoP 1949: 10); requiring eleven years of schooling and three years of BA (ibid., 11); and requiring school enrollment to increase to include 75 per cent children of school-going age (ibid., 11) are bandied every few years. However, even in 2004 none of the above stated goals have been achieved.

Proposals about quantity—creating academies, increasing educational institutions, creating new jobs (especially at the high level), establishing high-level institutions, chairs in foreign universities—were generally carried out. This is not surprising considering that these offices gave people high level jobs. And, of course, all bureaucracies tend to expand and especially at the higher level because this is where there is most money and power.

To monitor quantity, a study of the five year plans—the first plan being of December 1957—and the *Economic Survey of Pakistan* is necessary. Kaiser Bengali has carried out a brief survey of such plans (Bengali 1999). The first five-year plan (1955-60) set out to establish 4000 new schools in addition to 15,602 in existence. Moreover, school enrollment was to be increased to 1 million (from 43 to 49 per cent). The second, 1960-5, envisaged opening up 15,200 new primary schools in addition to the 18,000 in existence (only 2,400 were added earlier). The third, 1965-70, proposed setting up 42,500 schools in West Pakistan which would mean an additional enrollment of 2.8 million children in primary schools. The fifth plan, 1978-83, aimed at the enrollment of all boys in class-1 and increasing girls' enrollment from 33 to 45 per cent. The sixth plan of 1983-8, proposed the utilization of mosques as schools up to class-3; increasing enrollment from 48 to 75 per cent and launching a mass literacy programme covering 15 million persons. The seventh plan, 1988-93, proposed providing every child in the age group of 5 to 9 access to a school within a radius of 1.5 kilometers by 1992-93. The eighth plan of 1993-8, promised a primary school for a settlement of 300 people and a mosque school for smaller settlements. Moreover, the primary participation rate for boys was to be raised from 84.8 to 95.5 per cent and girls from 53 to 48 per cent. The perspective plan (1988-2003), given in chapter 2 of the seventh five year plan had the objective of eradicating 'illiteracy among youth—through full enrollment of the primary population' (p. 23). It was also proposed that 'the emphasis on educational and manpower planning will have to be shifted in favour of technical education and skill development—' (ibid., 25).

The targets laid out in each plan were generally not achieved as envisaged. However, much was achieved as far as the expansion of educational facilities is concerned. Despite the pressure of population, literacy has gone up from 16 per cent in 1951 to 51.6 per cent in 2003. During the same period the number of primary schools has gone up from 8000 to 170,000, and the enrollment in these from 0.77 million to 20 million (GoP 2003: 159). Examples of the failures are too numerous to enumerate. For instance, literacy was supposed to reach 100 per cent by 1975 but is still much less than the stated goal even today. The percentage of people (10 years and above) who are educated are 43.50 of the population and the enrollment ratio (as percentages of students to population 5.24 years) is 35.98 per cent. It is higher for males (41.19 per cent) and lower for females (30.35 per cent). It is more in the urban areas (49.71 per cent) and lower in the rural ones (29.11 per cent) (Census 2001: 120). The following table (Census 2001: 122) gives us an indication of the level of education of Pakistan's population.

Table 2.1

LEVEL	PERCENTAGE OF POPULATION
Below primary	18.30
Primary (class-5)	30.14
Middle (class-10)	20.89
Matriculation (class-10)	17.29
Intermediate (class-12)	6.56
Bachelor's (13 & 14 years of education)	4.38
Master's (15 & 16 years of education)	1.58
Others	0.44

The primary school children can read Urdu but understand no English. The matriculates know a little English but not enough to converse in it. Their knowledge of all other subjects is very sketchy and generally confined to information memorized in their textbooks. In the intermediate and bachelors levels, students confine themselves to such a stringent and impermeable academic division, or specialization as they call it, that they do not have much knowledge outside their narrow field. Master's students are also confined to their specialized field; moreover, they acquire knowledge through outdated and academically unsophisticated textbooks, guidebooks, and notes. The emphasis on quantity, though necessary, is not sufficient if a new direction, based on quality, is to be created.

As for other additions—the academies, chairs, institutes, and bureaucratic positions—the list is long and does not inspire confidence in the motives of the education decision makers. As mentioned earlier, such institutions benefit the elite—educational, bureaucratic and military—but do not fulfil the objectives they are meant to. In any case, these objectives were more political than educational and any keen observer could foretell that they would remain unfulfilled.

Besides the five-year plans, the educational policies provide us with guidelines of proposed policies in this regard. As mentioned earlier, the major policies were laid down in the 1950s. Among the major policy documents that appeared subsequently are: *Report of the Commission on National Education* (GoP 1959); *Report of the Commission on Student Problems and Welfare* (GoP 1966); *The New Education Policy* (GoP 1970); *The Education Policy* (GoP 1972); *National Educational Policy and implementation Programme* (GoP 1979 b); *National Education Policy* (GoP 1992); *National Education Policy 1998-2010* (GoP 1998) and *Education Sector Reforms* (GoP 2002 c).

Apart from the issues of quantity, which has been mentioned earlier, the policies bear looking at for other aspects of education. For instance, the 1959 report, considered a landmark in the field, launches an attack on the welfare concept of education:

> Good education is expensive, and educational expansion means more expense. The people must accept the fact that since it is they and their children who benefit most from education, the sacrifices required must be borne primarily by them (GoP 1959: 9).

This indicated a shift in governmental thinking, only too obvious now that quality education is almost entirely sold at exorbitant rates by the private sector or institutions of the state acting as private entrepreneurs. Ironically, however, the state continued to subsidize the education of the elite by establishing cadet colleges and elitist public schools throughout the country. This increased the gulf between the poor and the rich.

This document also created the Textbook Boards, which dominated education ever since (GoP 1959: 307). Their primary task was to ensure that the government's policies were reflected in the textbooks. These policies were:

1. 'The moral and spiritual values of Islam combined with the freedom, integrity, and strength of Pakistan should be the ideology which inspires our educational system' (ibid., 11).
2. 'We must strive to create a sense of unity and of nationhood among the people of Pakistan' (ibid., 11).

3. Imparting the 'skills and training necessary in a complex modern society' (ibid., 12).

Religious education, however, was more symbolic than real in the 'liberal' Ayub Khan era. While theology was introduced for Muslim children in the first eight years, it was not compulsory at higher levels, nor were sectarian differences conveyed to the students. As for the madrassas, Ayub Khan's government wanted them to teach secular subjects as well in order to incorporate them into the mainstream. This is what General Musharraf's government also ardently desires.

The 1959 report glossed over the issue of elite schooling, and it was precisely this issue which exploded in the face of the government in about six years or so. The government promulgated the University Ordinances in 1961, and in 1962 the students rose to agitate against it. Among other things they did not want a three-year B.A degree. But also, and significantly, they resented the elitist English-medium schools, which were mostly convent schools at that time, and wanted these to be abolished. Although the full story of this episode will be told in the chapter on English-medium schools, some facts need to be outlined here.

The Commission, which came to be called the Hamoodur Rahman Commission, defended the elite schools on the grounds that (a) they were very few as compared to the ordinary government schools; (b) they were run by private persons or Christian missionaries who have rights under the law to open schools and (c) that the state needs assistance by the private sector in opening schools.

The Commission, however, agreed that the government does spend more money on cadet colleges than on ordinary government schools, and that this contradicts the constitutional assurance against discrimination among citizens. It clearly said that the 'idea of superior and inferior schools does not fit in with our socio-economic pattern and the principles of equality and social justice as enunciated by Islam' (GoP 1966: 18). However, in the end, the privileged schools were saved through the suggestion that they should recruit students on 'merit' alone, and that 'mere poverty should not be a ground for exclusion' (ibid., 18). The fact that these schools are English-medium institutions and their entry tests would be biased against poor children who study in Urdu schools was not considered. Moreover, the fact that government itself subsidized and patronized elite schools—on whatever grounds—could not be explained away. And, indeed, because they were allowed to exist, they kept going about their business as usual, and even now cater to the elite of power and wealth in Pakistan.

On the whole, and ironically enough, although this report was written in response to students' agitation, it made no substantial concessions to them, except that the BA degree remained a course for two years. The faculties of the universities were subjected to increased bureaucratization. The report suggested:

> We notice that the commission on National Education suggested that confidential files of teachers should be maintained by the universities. We do not know if this recommendation has been implemented. If not, we strongly recommend that it should be done immediately in the manner suggested by the commission (GoP 1966: 83).

As for governance in the universities, the University Ordinances had already whittled away the power of the academics. As the report said:

> The system of nomination has been accepted in preference to election' in the governing bodies of the university. Moreover, 'very wide and extraordinary powers have been vested in the vice-chancellors including the power in some cases, as at Dacca and Rajshahi, to withhold implementation of the resolution of any body or authority of the university with which the vice-chancellor does not agree pending the decision of the chancellor (GoP 1966: 146).

Because of such laws, academics too had joined the students in their protest. Even at that time the major objections concerning governance were:

(1) That governors should not be chancellors of universities.
(2) The vice-chancellors should not be appointed by governors, but should be chosen out of a panel of eminent educationists prepared by the senate or syndicate.
(3) That the senate should be restored.
(4) That university authorities and bodies should consist of a majority of elected members.
(5) That universities should be fully autonomous bodies free from the control of government.
(6) That academic freedom should be assured to university teachers (adapted from GoP 1966: 148).

The report defended the ordinances on grounds that were reiterated again when objections to the Model University Ordinance (2002) were made: that high functionaries of the state can help universities in various ways; that the elective principle brings in people who politicize the campus and have a coterie of favourites during their tenure; that the senate, as a large body, is an arena for political conflict; that the state, which pays for the universities, should have some control on them (GoP 1966: chapter 12). However, the senate was restored with the proviso that it would be smaller and most of its members would be nominated.

While academics were subdued, students continued to resent Ayub Khan's autocratic regime. Some of this resentment fed into the movement against Ayub Khan in 1968. In 1969, when General Yahya Khan again imposed martial law, he too set about formulating an education policy. This time not a judge but a military officer, Air Marshal Nur Khan, was made its head. Significantly enough academics have not headed committees preparing education policies in Pakistan.

The New Education Policy (GoP 1970) hardly said anything new. There was the usual lip service to Islam about the need for 'the preservation and inculcation of Islamic values as an instrument of national unity and progress' (GoP 1970: 1). There was also the usual rhetoric about 'quality in education', 'academic freedom', and the role of education in the 'creation of a democratic social order by ensuring equal access to opportunities of education'. Nothing significantly new was proposed but the tone of the report was conciliatory rather than combative. Moreover, much to the relief of everybody concerned, the report was brief (26 pages) compared to the previous one (234 pages).

In a little less than two years the map of Pakistan had changed. After a war in December 1971 the province called East Pakistan became the independent country of Bangladesh. Zulfikar Ali Bhutto, who emerged as the elected leader of Pakistan, announced a new education policy that did not shift the broad parameters of the previous policies. However, there was an added emphasis on adult literacy. Also, and significantly, 3,334 private educational institutions were nationalized so that famous private colleges such as the Kinnaird College for Women, the Foreman Christian College in Lahore, and Gordon College in Rawalpindi were taken away from their former owners. It is reported that 1,828 schools, 346 madrassas, 155 colleges and 5 technical institutions were nationalized (GoP 1979: 26).

In most of these institutions the teachers were lowly paid and they welcomed nationalization, especially as the Pakistan Peoples Party government raised the salaries of college lecturers from class 2 to NPS 17, which was also the salary grade of civil service officers. However, the latter had extra benefits such as transport, phone, orderlies, office assistants and power, that the teachers did not possess. This egalitarian measure was much welcomed by the teachers though the critics said that a burden of Rs 15 crore per annum had to be borne by the state (GoP 1979b: 26). Apart from this, the education policy did not change much. Even now members of the university faculty who protest against the MUO (2002) want to go back to the University Act of 1973 despite the fact that it, too, ensures that real power in the university should not be with academics but with the government or its nominees.

Bhutto's government was dismissed by General Ziaul Haq in July 1977. Zia made a significant departure by putting in a real effort at Islamizing education. One major policy document called *National Education Policy and Implementation Programme* (GoP 1979b) declared that the foremost aims of education will be:

- To foster in the hearts and minds of the people of Pakistan in general and the students in particular a deep and abiding loyalty to Islam and Pakistan and a living consciousness of their spiritual and ideological identity thereby strengthening unity of the outlook of the people of Pakistan on the basis of justice and fairplay.
- To create awareness in every student that he, as a member of the Pakistani nation, is also a part of the universal Muslim Ummah and that it is expected of him to make a contribution towards the welfare of fellow Muslims inhabiting the globe on the one hand and to help spread the message of Islam throughout the world on the other.
- To produce citizens who are fully conversant with the Pakistan movement, its ideological foundations, history and culture so that they feel proud of their heritage and display firm faith in the future of the country as an Islamic state.
- To develop and inculcate in accordance with the Quran and Sunnah the character, conduct and motivation expected of a true Muslim (GoP 1979b: 1).

There are five other aims but only one is about strengthening scientific, vocational and technological education. This is how Ziaul Haq set out to 'Islamize the youth'.

Textbooks, which were supposed to be Islamized from 1947, were now given a religious orientation in most fields, even those of the natural sciences. Moreover, Islam was used to support the state's own militaristic policies in such a way that it appeared to the readers of these textbooks that Pakistan, the Pakistan movement, Pakistan's wars with India, the Kashmir issue were all connected not only with Pakistani nationalism but with Islam itself. Islamic studies was made compulsory up to class-10. There was much emphasis on Urdu, and for some time it appeared as if the English-medium schools would be banned. However, this did not happen and the private sector, which was encouraged to invest in education, built chains of schools catering to the fast expanding and more affluent middle class than existed earlier.

By the time Ziaul Haq died in 1988, children had to study Pakistan Studies and Islamic theology even up to the undergraduate level. The number of madrassas had multiplied and, as a consequence of the war in Afghanistan, they became increasingly militant. The number of elite English schools, and even institutions of higher learning, increased. Society was more clearly polarized along religious and class lines. Moreover, the increased awareness of religion, the lack of forums for expressing ideas freely, the increasing gap between the rich and the poor, had all contributed towards making this polarization potentially militant. This did happen but is in great danger of growing.

Ziaul Haq's government was followed by a so-called democratic interlude—so-called because the elected prime ministers were not very democratic and, in any case, the strongest power in the land remained in the hands of the army. Benazir Bhutto's and Nawaz Sharif's governments were dismissed by the then President with the support of the army. In the latest such incursion General Pervez Musharraf allowed elections to be held in October 2002 with Mir Zafarullah Khan Jamali appointed as the prime minister.

The education policy of these civilian governments did not change some of the fundamental features of the educational policy—such as Islamization, emphasis on the two-nation theory with its concomitant hatred for India, glorification of war and the military, subservience of teachers to administrators, increased control of the military and the private sector over elite education. But they did pay lip service to democracy throughout.

The ambitious policy document of Nawaz Sharif's days, *National Education Policy* 1998-2010 (GoP 1998) repeats the cliches every policy has been expounding, with differing emphases however, since 1947. Primary education was to be universalized by 2010 and more educational institutions would be created. A new feature was the emphasis on replacing the lecture method with computers, TV, video tapes etc. Apart from this, there was a whole chapter on 'Islamic Education' and it was declared that all aspects of education, including the sciences, are to be governed by religion (GoP 1998: 15). There is also a whole chapter (chapter 10) on information technology. The trend towards privatization, started by Ziaul Haq and promoted by all subsequent governments, was to be encouraged even further. It was estimated that about three million students were studying in about 10,000 English medium schools. Moreover, there were also five newly chartered private universities.

The producers of the report realized that the private sector could not be seen to share the burden of government: participation in education was already high in urban settlements. It was in the rural areas that more schools were needed. Thus, the role of the policy makers in universalization remained only marginal. Further, because of the use of English as medium of instruction, and high fees structure, these institutions were better suited to serve the requirement of the elite. Such a development is contradicted if effort is to be directed towards the development of an egalitarian society (GoP 1998: 134).

Nothing was actually done about the expensive private institutions, which kept multiplying and increasing their fees. The people of Pakistan appeared to have reconciled to paying exorbitant sums, making huge sacrifices and ransoming their old age pensions to pay for the education of their children. That this state of affairs will continue is clarified by the latest report, *Education Sector Reforms: Action Plan* 2001-2004 (GoP 2002c), issued during the rule of General Pervez Musharraf. It states that 'Private Sector investment in secondary and higher education is being promoted through liberal grant of charters, development of multiple textbooks and private exam boards' ('Foreword' by the Minister of Education, Zubaida Jalal). Otherwise, the reforms suggested are not different from those suggested in previous policies. There is the quantitative wish-list: literacy will go up from 49 to 60 per cent; primary enrollment from 66 to 76 per cent; middle school from 47.5 to 55 per cent; secondary school 29.5 to 40 per cent; and higher education from 2.6 to 5 per cent (ibid., 5). As for quality, the report mentions 'quality assurance' at a cost of 6.3 billion rupees, comprising curriculum reforms, teacher education, examination reforms and assessment (ibid., 35-36).

To sum up, one of the state's aims was to make education a vehicle for creating nationalism. This is an aim of all modern states, and especially ex-colonies of European powers, because nationalism has succeeded the royal dynasty as a principle of legitimizing power. What was wrong in Pakistan's case, however, is that the process of creating a nation involved the denial of the identity and rights of the ethnic entities whose willingness to stay together is the only guarantee of the strength of the federation and the creation of a unified Pakistani nation. Thus, the educational system denied ethnic diversity, and by doing so, it created further resentment and resistance to the idea of a Pakistani nation; an accommodating and just policy toward diverse ethnic groups would not have caused such bitterness. One cause, and perhaps a major one, of ethnicity was the inequality of the peripheral, less powerful, ethnic groups. Thus, the denial of ethnic identities, languages and cultures, through the educational system appeared as the perpetuation of inequality to ethnic activists and leaders in Pakistan.

The other dimension of inequality was linked with the three streams of education: the English-medium, the vernacular medium and the madrassa institutions. They catered, respectively, for the rich and the powerful; the deprived and the very poor and marginalized sections of the society.

As mentioned earlier the state or its various institutions, especially the military and the bureaucracy, have created educational institutions that cost more per student per year, and have used English rather than Urdu or any other language as medium of instruction. Thus the centre is privileged over the periphery as ethnic nationalists never tire of pointing out (see Amin 1988; Rahman 1996 and Ahmed 1998). Islamabad has better roads, better facilities and better educational institutions all at the taxpayer's expense. The Federal Directorate of Education, established in 1967, administers 396 educational institutions. Their cost per student per year is worked out as follows:

Federal Schools and Colleges

Type of Institutions	Number	Budget (2002-3)	Enrollment	Cost per Student per year
Schools	370	773,641,000	160576	4,818
Colleges	07	125,180,000	6674	18,756
Model Colleges	19	184,112,000	30,488	6,039

Source: Federal Directorate of Education, Islamabad.

NB: Model colleges, which are English-medium institutions, are schools as well as colleges. They have an evening shift also. The number of those in this shift in 2002-3 was 9,875 and has been included in the total given above.

The cost per student per year in these institutions can be seen to be higher than government schools and colleges in the Rawalpindi district and, for that matter, other institutions of a similar kind spread all over the country. In addition to the model colleges, some of the federal schools and colleges are also English-medium institutions, whereas provincial government schools are mostly Urdu-medium, and in some parts of Sindh, Sindhi-medium institutions.

Likewise, the armed forces have cantonments, garrisons and bases in almost all large urban areas of Pakistan. They have been, since the days of the British, the most well developed and fashionable parts of the cities. They, too, have better facilities than the old cities for the 'natives'. Besides influencing or controlling their own elite schools including the cadet colleges, the armed forces also control schools and colleges established by the federal government in the cantonments. The total number of such institutions in 2003 was 291 out of which 258 were schools and 33 colleges. The cost per student per year is as follows:

Army Schools and Colleges

Type of Institutions	Number	Budget (2002-3)	Enrollment	Cost per Student per year
Schools	258	668,904,000	1,75,883	3,803
Colleges	33	129,780,00	15,000	8,652

Source: Federal Government Educational Institutions (Cantonments and Garrisons) Directorate (Under Ministry of Defence).

Out of these, eighty-eight schools are English-medium institutions while the rest are Urdu-medium ones. The cost is higher in English-medium institutions though it cannot be calculated as the budget and enrollment for these schools is not available separately.

Not only did this class-based educational policy continue to thrive but with the rise of poverty, it became even more acute. Moreover, it spread upwards to higher education where the vernacular and English-medium streams used to meet. If the public-private ratio of enrollment increases from 85:10 to 60:40 by 2010, as envisaged in the latest education policy (GoP 2002 c: 48), inequality will become even more obvious. At the moment, in June 2003, there is much protest by school teachers and college lecturers against these policies. In short, as the state withdraws from education, educational apartheid increases. Exactly what are the features of this apartheid? Which institutions come about as a result of it? How much money, or lack of it, creates it? These are questions which the following pages intend to answer.

STORY

PROVIDING SCHOOLS FOR BALOCH GIRLS

I met Dr Qurat ul Ain Bakhteari on 24 February 2003 in Quetta. There was snow on the barren mountains walling Quetta City but the wind was not as freezing cold as I had imagined it would be. She walked in, graceful, smiling and very courteous in her welcome. We sat around dry fruit—the fabled almonds and pistachios of Afghanistan—while the gas heater spread its warmth in that spartanly furnished room with beautiful carpets. She had invited me to her brainchild, the Institute for Development Studies and Practice, to present a paper in a conference on language and globalization.

But somehow she started talking about the way she had established girls' schools in Balochistan. In doing so she had broken the myth that the Baloch do not allow women to be sent to school. The Baloch did send their daughters to school but the process was rather difficult. The major problem was to convince the girls' parents to send their daughter to school. She told me that she would go to the head of the household, often a grandfather, who let her go in to meet the women while he himself held court outside. Once inside the womens' quarters, the hierarchy was still an impediment in her quest for the girl's mother. For here sat the mater familias, the aged crone of a grandmother who would not let her meet the girl's mother without first grilling her for her own satisfaction. Qurat finally convinced the grandmother to let her go down the hierarchical ladder by talking about such down-to-earth things as the time the girl got up, the breakfast she would have and the clothes she would wear to school. At this the grandma had to suggest that she had better talk to the girl's mother. This is exactly what Qurat wanted and so she would convince the parents to send their daughter to the school. Moreover, she would also find out how many girls there were in the village. Meanwhile, her male colleague was enacting the same drama to reach the girl's father before the watchful eyes of the pater familias.

The parents then formed the village education committee without offending influential elders. They ran the schools without outside help initially. However, when the school did take off, government officials came and started paying a salary to the teachers. Later a building was added, the teaching material came in and a collaborative school was ready.

Dr Qurat began this work in 1992 and remained the Director of the Balochistan Primary Education Development Programme till 1998. This whole experience has been described by Shahla Haeri in her detailed interview of Qurat in *No Shame for the Sun* (2002: 47-106). However, I have taken Qurat's own description of it on that winter evening when I had the pleasure of meeting her (Haeri, 2002).

3

URDU-MEDIUM SCHOOLS

According to the *Pakistan Integrated Household Survey* [PIHS] (2001-2002) the net enrollment rate, i.e. the number of students enrolled in primary schools divided by the total number of children in that age group, is 42 per cent (PIHS). Even more alarming is the fact that the poorer one is, the less chances there are of obtaining any education at all. The poorest people, described as the 1st quintile in the PIHS, manage to send 27 per cent children to school, while the richest, called the 5th quintile, send 56 per cent to school. (PIHS 2002).[1] Moreover, households spend Rs 1,443 a year on a primary school student while those sending a child to a private school spend four times more (ibid.: Table 2.21 and p. 14). This expenditure includes uniform, books, stationery and transport. The expensive elitist English-medium schools, which are only a small percentage of the 38,893 private schools surveyed by the Ministry of Education in 2000 (Census Private 2001: Table 1, p. 12), charge tuition and admission fees between Rs 18,000 to 50,000 per year. If one adds the expenditure on books, stationery, uniform, transport and other things the expenditure rises to much higher figures.

This indicates that the Pakistani educational scene is polarized according to socio-economic class. As one indicator of the cost of schooling is the medium of instruction it may be said that the vernacular-medium schools (Urdu, Sindhi and Pashto-medium) are meant for the working classes and the lower middle classes. The English-medium schools are meant for the middle and upper classes. This distinction is well known and the proposals for the educational policy of 1969, associated with Air Marshal Nur Khan, stated categorically that there was 'almost a caste-like distinction between those who feel at ease in expressing themselves in English and those who do not' (GoP 1969: 14).

This chapter is about one caste—that which studies in the Urdu-medium schools—in our system of educational apartheid.

The Urdu-medium schools are the largest in number, and the most significant, since all ordinary government schools in Karachi, parts of Hyderabad, Balochistan, NWFP, Azad Kashmir and Punjab are Urdu-medium institutions. As for the vernacular-medium schools, the Pashto-medium ones run only up to class–5, after which students go to Urdu-medium schools. The Sindhi-medium schools operate only in parts of Sindh. Thus the most representative schools for ordinary people are those that are Urdu-medium. These, therefore, are the ones which have been studied.

The number of all government schools is given as follows in the *Economic Survey of Pakistan* (GoP 2003):

good

Table 3.1
Government Schools in Pakistan

Level	Number	Students Strength	Teachers
Primary	164,200	19,521,000	335,100
Middle	19,100	3,938,000	101,200
Secondary	12,900	1,704,000	165,000

Source: GoP 2003: 105-106.

These numbers include Sindhi-medium government schools also. The number of these, however, was 36,750 in 1998. The Pashto-medium primary schools were 10,731 in 1999 (field research). Thus, most of these schools are Urdu-medium.

These students and teachers both come from the lower-middle class. *Ref* In a small survey of 230 students and 100 teachers of Urdu-medium schools undertaken in December 2002 and January 2003, it was discovered that they belonged to the low-income groups. They were reluctant to reveal their family income because of the social stigma of poverty and 95 people (41.30 per cent) did not report their father's income. As for mothers, most of them did not have paid employment so that 220 (95.65 per cent) did not report their income. Out of those who did, most (60.74 per cent) belonged to the poorer classes (working and lower middle classes) (see Annexure 1). The teachers of these schools also belong to the same class or to the lower middle class (65.96 per cent).

After ten years of schooling, students sit for examinations held by the different Boards of Intermediate and Secondary Education in the country. The teaching and the examinations are both in Urdu except in parts of (mostly rural) Sindh where they are in Sindhi.

Schools are not accessible to all children; they are often too far from where the children live. Therefore, children must spend a considerable amount of time, energy, and money to get to school. According to the PIHS (2002) most children travel less than 2 kms and a few even travel more than 5 kms to their schools. However, girls do have to travel long distances in Balochistan and Sindh, which is difficult and unsafe for them.

Schools are generally dull, stringent places, often painted a dirty yellow with blue doors and windows with broken glass panes. They are highly regimented with semi-educated teachers forcing their pupils to memorize passages out of poorly written, poorly printed and extremely dull books. Classrooms are overcrowded with forty-one girls and thirty-eight boys per teacher in the primary schools of all provinces except Balochistan. In Balochistan, the most deprived province of all, there are forty-eight girls per teacher (PIHS 2002).

INFLUENCES OF TEXTBOOKS ON URDU-MEDIUM SCHOOL STUDENTS

Textbooks are one of the many influences on a person's worldview. How significant the influence may be depends on many variables— teachers, peer pressure, family and friends, childhood experiences, exposure to discourses other than textbooks—and it cannot be easily determined. What can be determined, however, is the intention of the writers of textbooks; the policy guidelines of those who get the textbooks written; and the values which the educational authorities responsible for writing and disseminating textbooks in educational systems support.

In general these values belong to the 'in-group' i.e. they are values and perceptions that support one's own group— nation, ethnic group, religious group, ideological group etc. This necessitates the creation of an 'out-group' or 'other' which must be held in opposition to the self. The 'other' is generally created on the basis of selective data, and in this process of creation it is transformed. It may either be romanticized or demonized. Edward Said in his book *Orientalism* (1978) tells us how European scholars of the Orient created an image of the 'Other', which made it the 'Other' of the Occident. Said further postulates that this justified the conquest of the Orient in order to 'civilize' it.

Most of the 25,995,068 (GoP 2002: 146) students who are from Urdu-medium schools, study the textbooks provided by the Textbook Boards of the four provinces of Pakistan. Ethnicity is ignored to create a Pakistani identity, although these centrist policies have been resented by ethnic communities and have resulted in the creation of Bangladesh in 1971. Still the textbooks reinforce these (for ethnic politics see Amin 1988; Rahman 1996 and Ahmed 1998). There is also much glorification of war and the military and many anti-Hindu and anti-India remarks and religious bias interspersed throughout the books (for detailed analysis see Aziz 1993; Hoodbhoy and Nayyar 1985; Saigol 1995; and Rahman 2002: 515-524. For a comparison between the history textbooks of India and Pakistan see Kumar 2001). The latest analysis of Pakistani school textbooks is found in a report entitled *The Subtle Subversion* (Nayyar and Salim 2003) which was hotly debated in March-April 2004. As it became a bone of contention between the liberals and the conservatives (both the Islamists and the security conscious establishment) the government of Prime Minister Jamali stopped the implementation of the report.

THE OBJECTIVES OF THE STATE

The government of Pakistan lays down certain objectives for the teaching of various subjects. These are often ideological. They use Islam as a marker of identity to define the boundaries of the self. The 'other' is, by definition, non-Muslim. However, this notion of Islam is so tempered with nationalism as to exclude Indian Hindus rather than non-Muslims who are friendly with Pakistan. Here is an abstract from the objectives laid down in different instructional books from the Ministry of Education.

Table 3.2

SOCIAL STUDIES

- To inculcate the unflinching love for Islam and Pakistan, strong sense of national cohesion, and state integrity.
- To promote understanding of socio-economic and socio-cultural aspects of Pakistani society, the Ideology of Pakistan and struggle for freedom. (GoP 2002a).

History of Pakistan

- To evaluate the Islamization effort by various Governments in perspective of an Islamic ideological framework.
- To inculcate among students the qualities of Khudi, self-reliance, tolerance, research, sacrifice, Jihad, martyrdom, modesty and the behaviour patterns of national character. (GoP 2002b).

These objectives appear to counteract the ostensibly secularization trend of General Musharraf's government. Indeed, they are quite similar to the Islamization trend of the Zia regime. In short, the use of Islam to define the self and mark out the 'Other' has not changed. Because of this Pakistani students exposed to the Textbook Board books tend to be intolerant of Hindus, Christians and non-Muslim minorities.

ANALYSIS OF THE PUNJAB TEXTBOOK BOARD SCHOOL TEXTBOOKS

The following case study of some of the recently (2002) published books of the Punjab Textbook Board, Lahore, is being undertaken here for the first time. The earlier books have been analyzed by the author and others in different contexts but not specifically with reference to the images of the 'Other'.

Table 3.3
Images of the 'Other' in English Textbooks

Class-6	There are sentences like 'I am a Muslim. I am a Pakistani'. However, no adverse comment against Hindus or Christians appears in the book.
Class-7	No adverse comments on any religious group. Girls are clad in scarves (*dopattas*), which cover the hair.
Class-8	No adverse comments. No negative image.
Class-9	A statement: 'Islam was a dominant force in Spain for about eight hundred years' (p. 84), implicitly glorifies Muslim rule over Christian Spain.
Class-10	An essay on Tariq bin Ziad, the conqueror of Spain, justifies his conquest.
Conclusion:	English textbooks generally do not portray the 'Other' (non Muslims) adversely but Islamic rule over the West is justified.

Table 3.4
Images of the 'Other' in Urdu Textbooks

Class-6	An Urdu couplet which in English translation reads as follow. 'The Himalaya remembers their (the Muslims') deeds. Gibraltar still carries their stamp on it' (p. 24). In an essay on the 1965 Pakistan-India War: 'clever and manipulative enemy' (for India) (p. 68).
Class-7	In praise of the poet Akbar Ilahabadi: 'He was against Western culture in India'. Anti-Hindu remarks: 'In those days the extremist Hindus had launched a movement against Urdu since they considered it the Muslims' Language' (p. 137).
Class-8	With reference to the partition in 1947: 'The Hindus and Sikhs killed Muslims whenever they were in a minority. They burnt their houses and forced them to migrate to Pakistan' (p. 46). About an Indian pilot: 'In the other world he had to burn; here too he died by fire'.
Class-9	Romanticizing Muslim rule over India: 'The Muslims ruled South Asia for about a thousand years. They treated their Hindu subjects with justice. However, the Hindus would revolt at the least opportunity' (p. 11).

(*Continued*)

The conspiratorial Hindus had a large share in harming Tipu Sultan and Siraj ud Dowlah—.

When the English consolidated their rule, the Hindus openly sided with them—because both hated the Muslims—Hindus are ready to change for their advantage—they made a plan to enslave the Muslims permanently' (p. 12).

Conclusion: Urdu textbooks portray the Hindus, and to a lesser degree the colonial British, very negatively. Hindus are accused of being cunning, deceptive and scheming and are accused of hating the Muslims. Both the British and the Hindus are supposed to have conspired together to deprive the Muslims of their rights. (The 'Other' is always non-Muslim).

Table 3.5
SOCIAL STUDIES

Class-7

(English version)
'The people of Africa requested the Muslims to invade their lands to save them from the tyranny of their Christian rulers who extorted taxes from them' (p. 21)
This essay refers to the Muslim conquest of foreign lands with pride (p. 22).

Class-8   'As a result of Hindu-British collusion, Muslims were subjected to great hardships — they could not be cowed down by the atrocities committed on them by the British and the Hindus' (p. 73).
'Both the communities [British and Hindus] conspired against the Muslims to turn them into a poor, helpless and ineffective minority' (p. 74).
On the crusades: 'They [Christians] wanted to revenge themselves on Muslims—the Christians took to their traditional tactics of conspiring against the ruler' (p. 27).
On colonialism:—European nations have been working during the past three centuries, through conspiracies or naked aggression to subjugate the countries of the Muslim world' (p. 43).
Anti-Hindus remarks: 'The Quaid-i-Azam saw through the machinations of the Hindus' (p. 51).
'The ignoble behaviour of the Hindus forced the Muslims to rally to the Muslims League Flag to get their demands conceded—the Hindus had treated the Muslims cruelly and shamefully during their rule' (p. 82).

(Continued)

Class-9
and 10   In Bengal Haji Shariat Ullah and Tito Mir started the struggle to
            free the Muslims from the slavery of the English and the Hindus
            (p. 13).

Conclusion: Social studies textbooks strongly reinforce the conspiracy theory
            that the Hindus and the colonial British wanted to suppress the
            Muslims and keep them in perpetual slavery. They romanticize
            and glorify Muslim rule over Hindus and Western people (who
            are always the 'Other').

In a previous study of 1999 of all language and literature Textbook
Board books from class-1 to class-10, the present author counted
ideology-carrying items. They were divided under three main headings:
Pakistani nationalism, Islam and the military. Under the first heading
were all items—prose lessons, poems, exercises etc—about the
Pakistan movement, nationalist heroes, messages on national
integration, Pakistani identity, ideology of Pakistan etc. Under the
second were items relating to religious personages, beliefs and
movements. Under the last were articles about war, Pakistan's wars
with India, war heroes, glorification of the military etc. The following
chart gives the consolidated data for the textbooks of different
languages:

Table 3.6
Language-wise Ideological Contents of Language Textbooks
**Expressed as percentages of total items (i.e. poems, prose pieces,
exercises etc.)**

Language	Content (in percentages)
Arabic	66
Urdu	40
Pashto	43
Persian	32
Sindhi	29
English	8

Source: Physical counting of all items in the textbooks of all provinces in 1998. For
        details see Rahman (2002) pp. 519-522.

As Arabic, Pashto and Persian are optional languages, and Sindhi is studied only in Sindh, Urdu emerges as the main ideology-carrying language. It influences all, except madrassa students, since even English-medium school students have to study this language. However, as English-medium students are exposed to other discourses that probably dilute the influence of the state-sponsored ideological texts, it is only the Urdu-medium ones (i.e. the common people of Pakistan) who face the full brunt of this ideological exposure.

It should be added that lessons are taught through rote learning in crammed classes where the teacher is authoritative and, indeed, very intimidating. The teacher often makes a child recite the lesson in a sing-song voice (*ek dooni dooni; do dooni char*) and the class joins in the chorus. Children rock their bodies as they chant the familiar parroted formulas. This happens not only in recitation of arithmetical tables but, indeed, it is the major method of instruction. Essays in languages are written on the black board to be copied verbatim. Any originality, any questioning of given facts, any deviation from the traditional interpretation is frowned upon and sometimes punished. Actually, what will become clear later in the context of madrassa education, the Urdu-medium schools continue the tradition of the madrassa which functioned in a society in transition from orality to literacy (hence the use of mnemonic devices, repetition, chorus etc.), and one which had to conserve the sacred texts and their orthodox interpretations from the irreverent attacks of the heretics (hence the intolerance of questioning and analytical analysis leading to new results).

Thus, while the British implanted modern education in India, Pakistanis adapted it to time-honoured cultural norms, creating a hybrid between madrassa and modern education.

FUNDING OF URDU SCHOOLS

These schools employ matriculates to teach primary classes and those with FA and BA degrees to teach middle and high schools classes. The salaries given to the teachers in most schools are as follows:

Table 3.7

Educational Level	Salary Grade	Average pay & allowances per month
Matriculation	7	7,578
FA (CT)	10	8,448
BA (B.Ed.)	16	14,099
Headmaster	17	18,316

The budget of an Urdu-medium Federal Government Model School in Islamabad, even though better paid than its provincial counterparts, was a total of Rs 5, 309,000 for the year 2002-3. As there were 960 boys in this school, the expenditure per pupil per year is expected to be Rs 5,530. According to the figures given by the Federal Directorate of Education (Islamabad) the cost per student per year is Rs 4,818 (in 370 schools the enrollment is 160,576 whereas the budget for 2002-3 is Rs 773,641,000). The major heads of expenditure are given in detail in Annexure-7 which indicate that there are some matriculate and intermediate pass teachers on the faculty of even government schools in cities. In the rural areas the number of below-graduate teachers is very high.

The average expenditure per pupil per year in ordinary Urdu-medium government schools can be judged by looking at the schools of the Rawalpindi district in 2003.

Table 3.8
Cost Per Pupil Per Year in Urdu-Medium Government Schools in 2003
(Rawalpindi District)

	Male	Female	Total
Schools	1,191	1,213	2,404
Enrollment	389,259	170,696	559,955
Teachers	7,236	6,073	13,309
Teachers/student ratio	54 students per teacher	28 per teacher	42 per teacher

(Continued)

Budget			Rs 1268 million
Cost per pupil per year	-	-	Rs 2,264.5
Cost to the state (per pupil per year)	-	-	Rs 2,264.5

Source: Office of the District Executive Officer (Education), Rawalpindi.

Recently, because of the dismal state of government schools, philanthropists and social workers have started establishing schools. There are many examples of such initiatives, but only one well-known example is mentioned here. The Citizens Foundation, which set up its first school in Karachi in 1995, is a 'not-for-profit organization run by businessmen and professionals.' It runs '76 primary schools, 24 secondary schools, one teacher training unit as well as an information technology institute. With more than 18,000 children from *katchi abadis* enrolled at TCF schools in 17 cities, the organization is clearly bent on making a difference' (Hussain 2003: 89). In these schools the tuition fees is Rs 100 per month, which makes them out of the reach of the poorest people anyway. However, the donors pay the rest of the cost per students which comes to Rs 5000 per year—like that of the best government schools which are almost free.

While it is true that philanthropists are needed to help the government, the problem is that the government is giving up on education. After all, providing hopelessly inadequate education in government schools, and that too only in the urban areas, is tantamount to giving up on good and equal education for all citizens.

CONDITIONS IN URDU SCHOOLS

The low salaries, which these schools offer attracts only those who fail to get other jobs. Thus the quality of instruction in most schools catering to the common people is very low. The classrooms are bare and in rural areas classes are often held outdoors because of lack of space. There is no heating or air conditioning though, in the cities, the headmaster's office is sparsely furnished. The teachers, at least in boy's schools, often carry canes and corporal punishment is allowed to be administered. This, in fact, is a major reason why children tend to drop out of school.

Just as the poorest children have the lowest enrollment in schools, they also tend to drop out more than others. Thus, 53 per cent of the poorest quintile dropped out before completing class 6 compared with only 23 per cent of the richest quintile (HID 2002: 15). Parents and teachers explain this as due to lack of motivation as do teachers. This shifts the burden of failure on to the pupil. However, if one considers the extremely harsh conditions at home and the cruel treatment children receive at school, one wonders why more do not drop out.

OTHER INFLUENCES ON URDU-MEDIUM STUDENTS

Since Urdu-medium students are from the upper-working and lower-middle class backgrounds, they are less exposed to Western discourses available on cable television, English books and conversations of peer group members, family and friends who have been abroad. Their families are conservative and religious as Jasmin Mirza, a sociologist working on transformation of norms governing gender-specific behaviour in Lahore, mentions in relation to women (Mirza 2002). The Urdu newspapers that their family reads or hears being read out in the bazaar, are also conservative and religious. Their teachers, who are from the same socio-economic class, reinforce the ideas otherwise disseminated by the Urdu press (see the views of teachers given below), school textbooks, Pakistani official radio and television, families and the peer group. These ideas—the worldview of the lower middle classes in Pakistan—favour the Islamization of the state though they do not favour rule by the clergy. This is often explained by saying that maulvis are harsh, or corrupt, or not aware of modern ideas but that Islam, if implemented in its true spirit by honest and enlightened leaders, can solve all social problems.

A corollary of this Islamic outlook is emotionality about religious issues and, hence, intolerance for the religious 'other', i.e. the Hindu, the Ahmedi[2] and, to a lesser degree, the Christian. Part of this emotion has also been transferred to Pakistani nationalism. Indeed, the use of religious symbolism to sacralize the Pakistan movement, the wars with India and particularly the Kashmir dispute with India, has been partly successful though students seem to be aware that an open war with India would be disastrous. Thus teachers, parents and the peer group reinforce chauvinistic views in this socio-economic class in the urban centres of the NWFP, Punjab and to some extent in Karachi.

MILITANCY AND TOLERANCE AMONG URDU-MEDIUM SCHOOL STUDENTS AND TEACHERS

In the recent survey of 230 students and 100 teachers of Urdu-medium schools responses to questions about militancy in Kashmir and giving equal rights to Ahmedis (a sect declared as a non-Muslim minority in 1974 in Pakistan), Pakistani Hindus and Christians and women were tabulated as percentages. These students and teachers both come from the lower-middle class as their income indicates.

The questions given to samples of students and teachers in December 2002 and January 2003 were meant to find out whether they supported militant policies in Kashmir as students from these schools did in 1999. There were also questions to find out whether religious minorities should be given the same rights as Muslim citizens of Pakistan. There was also a question about giving equal rights to men and women. The questions about Kashmir were as follows:

Table 3.9
Militancy Among Urdu-medium School Students (N=230)
(in percentages)

WHAT SHOULD BE PAKISTAN'S PRIORITIES?			
	Yes	No	Don't Know
1. Take Kashmir away from India by an open war?	39.56	53.04	7.39
2. Take Kashmir away from India by supporting Jihadi groups to fight with the Indian army?	33.04	45.22	21.74
3. Support Kashmir case through peaceful means only (i.e. no open war or sending Jihadi groups across the line of control)	75.65	18.26	6.09

Source: Survey 2003 (Annexure 2).

The responses of the teachers of these schools (N=100) to the same questions are as follows:

Table 3.10
Militancy Among Urdu-medium School Teachers
(in percentages)

WHAT SHOULD BE PAKISTAN'S PRIORITIES?	Yes	No	Don't Know
1. Open war	20	70	10
2. Jihadi Groups	19	68	13
3. Peace	85	10	05

Source: Annexure 2.

The survey indicates that there has been a shift away from supporting militancy in the Urdu-medium schools since my last survey of school students in 1999 (Rahman 2002: Appendix 14). However, since the questions this time clearly spelled out the possibility of war or proxy war whereas only the emotive and romantic term 'conquer' was used last time, the response this time is realistic and pragmatic. It is also possible that since Pakistan and India have come to the brink of war several times since 1999 when the last survey was carried out, the attitude of respondents towards war is less macho and 'gung-ho'. Moreover, since General Pervez Musharraf himself reversed the policy of carrying out a covert war in Kashmir and has talked of averting war, students and teachers might have felt that it was safer and perhaps more desirable not to support war. Thus there is less support of militant policies now then there was in 1999-2000.

However, the level of tolerance for the religious minorities is not very high, at least for the Ahmedis and the Hindus. However, it is quite high for Christians and very high for women. The relevant questions and their responses are as follows:

Table 3.11
Tolerance Among Urdu-medium school students
2002-2003 (N=230)
(In percentages)

What should be Pakistan's priorities?

	Yes	No	Don't Know
1. Give equal rights to Ahmedis in all jobs etc?	46.95	36.95	16.09
2. Give equal rights to Pakistani Hindus in all jobs etc?	47.39	42.61	10
3. Give equal rights to Pakistani Christians in all jobs etc?	65.65	26.52	7.83
4. Give equal rights to men and women as in Western Countries?	75.22	17.39	7.39

Source: Annexure 2.

The questions in the survey of 1999-2000 were essentially the same though, unfortunately, questions (2) and (3) had been lumped into one question. The responses to these are reproduced below:

Table 3.12
Tolerance Among Urdu-medium School Students
1999-2000 (N=510)
(In percentages)

	Yes	No	Don't Know
1. Give Ahmedis (or Mirzais) the same rights (jobs, opportunities etc) as others in Pakistan.	44.04	33.85	22.12
2. Give Hindus and Christians the same rights as others in Pakistan	56.73	23.65	19.62
3. Give equal rights to women	84.81	9.04	6.15

Source: Survey 2000 in Rahman 2002: Appendix 14.6.

The tolerance towards women appears to be less now but that is probably because the question specifies that the equal rights are those available in Western countries. Even so some respondents ticked 'Yes' adding 'equal as defined by Islam'.

The responses of the teachers to the same questions are as follow:

Table 3.13
Tolerance of Religious Minorities and Women in Urdu-medium
among School Teachers 2002-2003
(N=100) (In percentages)

	Yes	No	Don't Know
1. Ahmedis	27	65	08
2. Hindus	37	58	05
3. Christians	52	42	06
4. Women	61	33	06

Source: Annexure 2.

In short, the teachers are actually less tolerant of religious minorities and do not support equal rights for men and women despite the fact that out of the 100 teachers in the sample, 58 were women and 42 were men. The gender-wise break down of opinions reveals how intolerant men were of the idea of women having the same rights as them (figures are in percentages):

Table 3.14
Gender-wise Tabulation of Attitudes Towards Equality of Men
and Women among Urdu-Medium Schools Teachers
(In percentages)

Give equal rights to men and women as in Western countries?			
	Yes	No	Don't Know
Men (N=42)	35.71	54.76	9.52
Women (N=58)	79.31	17.24	3.45

Source: Annexure 2.1.

The opinions of parents have not been obtained through questionnaires but observation suggests that in the lower middle class, which is where the teachers and students of Urdu-medium schools come from, they too express opinions similar to the teachers.

Conclusion

In short, if one is to hazard an informed guess about the influence of the teachers of the Urdu-medium schools, and parents, upon the students it is that both express intolerant opinions about the religious minorities in Pakistan. They also glorify the role of the army though certain military rulers, viewed as secular , are not approved of. They also express highly biased views about India, which is always called 'Hindu' India, and feel that the West, especially the United States, is a friend of India and against Muslims. Such views are very commonly expressed in the Urdu press, especially in *Nawa-i-Waqt*, and can be heard among lower-middle and middle-class people.

Despite the predominance of such views not all children are brainwashed into believing them to the exclusion of other opinions. Similarly, despite the rote-learning forced upon students, not all of them lack analytical skills later in life. And despite English being a formidable barrier—more students fail in it than in other compulsory subjects (see Annexure 3)— some students learn it and enter the highest services in Pakistan and abroad. This speaks highly of the motivation and innate abilities of the successful students but it should be kept in mind that they succeed in spite of the system not because of it.

STORY

URDU SCHOOL CHILDREN

I met Shahzad Hussain (not his real name) in an Urdu-medium school in a town near Rawalpindi. He was wearing the *shalwar qameez* uniform of the school and his satchel was bursting with books. I asked him whether I could talk to him about his life and he nodded his head but did not say a word. My questions were answered with monosyllables and nods and shakes of the head.

As it happened, I went to the school again to find out its budget and the boy himself came forward to shake my hand with a welcoming smile. This time, during the break, he told me that his father was a peon in a government office. He walked one kilometer to the school daily accompanied by his father whose office was also near the school. He was doing well in his studies but found English an incomprehensible and deeply mystifying subject. His strategy was to learn each lesson by heart and recite it in a sing-song voice much as he recited the holy book, which too he did not understand. His other fright was the Maulvi Sahib who taught him Islamiyat. The Maulvi Sahib had a stick the boys called Maula Baksh and the said Maula Baksh loved nothing better than making boys howl with pain. But the bad time was over and the matriculation examination was drawing near. Shahzad wanted to go to the college and maybe to become a doctor one day.

Had he been a girl and in a far off village the future could hardly have been so rosy. In one village a mother of girls confessed that she was afraid her girls would be abducted on the way as they were rather comely. Another mother said she did not send the children to school because she was too poor to afford the soap needed to wash the uniform and, more importantly, how could she press it every day? Electricity did not exist and coal for the iron was expensive. Even more heartbreaking was the case of the mother who said she could not afford the lunch. At home the children made do with whatever was available. At school, however, they had to compete with other children and wouldn't the family lose face if they ate only onions with dry bread for lunch?

And yet, the sheer population pressure fills the schools even when they are running both in the morning and the evening. That is why very poor children are sent to the madrassas and those whose parents have some money send them to so-called English-medium schools that are found in every city and town of Pakistan.

4

ENGLISH-MEDIUM SCHOOLS

All over the cities of Pakistan, one can see billboards advertising institutions proclaiming to be English-medium schools or tuition 'centres' claiming to teach spoken English and English for passing all kinds of examinations and interviews. These are seen in areas ranging from the most affluent to slums and even in the rural areas. Indeed, most of them are located in middle-class, lower-middle-class and even in working-class areas than in the more affluent localities of the cities. Except in the claim made by the billboards, they share little else in common. They are a far cry from the rolling green grounds of Aitchison College in Lahore to a two-room house in a slum that advertises itself as the 'Oxford and Cambridge Islamic English-medium School'. Indeed, if there is anything which links such diverse establishments together it is that they cater to the persistent public demand for English education. English is still the key to a good future—a future with human dignity if not public deference; a future with material comfort if not prosperity; a future with that modicum of security, human rights and recognition, that all human beings desire. So, irrespective of what the state provides, parents are willing to part with scarce cash to buy their children such a future.

The English-medium schools are of three major types: (a) state-influenced elitist public schools, (b) private elitist schools and (c) non-elitist schools. Within each category are sub-categories. Indeed, the non-elitist English-medium schools are so varied that they defy classification. Let us, however, focus only on the major categories in order to understand what type of inequality exists in them.

The state-influenced institutions are the top public schools and cadet colleges, the federal government model schools, and the armed forces schools. While most of the cadet colleges and public schools are elitist institutions, some of the federal government and other schools of state institutions are not elitist. For the purposes of classification in the

Fee as criteria for classification

survey of such institutions that I carried out in 1999-2000, I included institutions charging tuition fees of Rs 1500 per month and above as elitist institutions. Ordinary government schools have tuition fees ranging between Rs 2-25 per month while private and state-controlled non-elitist English schools, or ordinary English-medium schools as they have been called in this survey, charge tuition fees ranging between Rs 50-1499 per month. There is, however, another complication. In the schools run by institutions—the armed forces, customs, PIA, telephone and telegraph, universities—the tuition fees is less for children of the employees or beneficiaries and more for other children. In such cases I have taken the fees paid by non-beneficiaries as the criterion in the survey of opinion of students. As this survey was published in *Language Ideology and Power* (2002: Appendix 14), it has not been used here. I have, however, referred to it at places. For this chapter, however, I did carry out a survey in March-April 2003 of the faculty and students of elitist English-medium schools and cadet colleges/public schools (see Annexure 2). First, however, let us look at the history of English-medium elitist schools in South Asia.

HISTORICAL BACKGROUND

Under British rule, there were two kinds of elitist schools in India: those for the hereditary aristocracy, called the Chiefs' Colleges; and those for the newly emerging professional classes, called European or English schools (including English-teaching schools and armed forces schools that taught all subjects in English). Both kinds of institutions served political and social purposes. The Chiefs' Colleges were meant to anglicize young rulers, to encourage loyalty to the crown, and preclude events like those of 1857. This was the principle of 'indirect rule' discussed by J.M. Mangan in some detail in the context of schooling (1986: 125). In keeping with the 'white man's burden' theory, the idea was, as Captain F.K.M. Walter—the agent of the Bharatpur Agency—put it in his report of 1869-70, to 'establish an Eton in India' to help the princes come up to the level of the British and thus become 'promoters of peace, prosperity and progress among their own peoples and hearty supporters of British authority' (in Mangan 1986: 125). Six major 'Chiefs' Colleges' were established: Rajkumar College (1870) at Rajkot; Mayo College (1872) at Ajmer;

for Rajputana; Rajkumar College (1871) Nowgong for Bundelkhand; Daly College (1876) at Indore for Central India; and Aitchison College at Lahore (1886) for the chiefs of the Punjab. There were lesser schools for the landed gentry too, the most notable among them being: Colvin Taluqedar School, Lucknow; Rajkumar College, Raipur; Nizam College, Hyderabad; Taluqedar School at Sadra, Gujrat; etc (PEI 1918: 183-5; Mangan 1986: 126-7). Here the emphasis was on English as the central symbol and tool in the process of Anglicization. Lord Curzon, the Viceroy of India (1898-1905), believed that the young chiefs who were supposed to 'learn the English language, and [become] sufficiently familiar with English customs, literature, science, mode of thought, standards of truth and honour', would be allies of the British (Raleigh 1906: 245). The assumption that these English values and norms of conduct were intrinsically superior was, of course, part of Curzon's worldview, as it was of most Englishmen. The political motive of making the chiefs loyal to the Crown and so consolidating the empire was justified on the assumption that it was morally necessary to civilize Indians.

Accordingly, between 1897 and 1902, English was taught on an average of nine out of a total of twenty-five hours in classes one and two at Aitchison College. In the other Chiefs' Colleges too, it was given more teaching hours than any other subject (Mangan 1986: 131). The Chiefs' Colleges, patronized by eminent members of the ruling elite (including governors and the Viceroy), had imposing buildings, excellent facilities for games and sports, paid high salaries to their British administrators (Rs 1,250 per month to the Principal of Mayo College), and charged very high tuition fees from their pupils (Rs 4,300 per year at Mayo and Rs 1,250 at Aitchison) (Mangan 128-31). Such exorbitant education costs excluded all but the wealthiest from such institutions.

Children of the newly emerging professional upper middle class Indian families sought admission in the European schools. Here too, because such schools admitted only 15 per cent Indians (except in Bombay where 20 per cent were allowed), not everybody could get in. The schools which admitted more than 20 per cent Indian students were called English-teaching schools (PEI 1918: 185). These schools generally granted the Senior School Certificate to pupils at the end of their schooling. According to Sharp, this certificate is 'in the opinion of those who have had long experience of both systems of examination, equal to an ordinary degree of the University of Calcutta' (PEI 1918:

180). Such high educational standards did not prevail in the Chiefs' Colleges (where the pupils did not have to compete for jobs) though they were much improved by reforms instituted by Lord Curzon and his successors in the first two decades of the twentieth century (Mangan 140-1).

The English schools—to choose a convenient term for all such institutions that taught most subjects through English—were generally run on the lines of British public schools, whether the administrators were missionaries or others. In the area now comprising Pakistan, such schools existed only in the big cities. In the NWFP, for instance, it was reported in 1938 that 'the Convent Day School is the major English school and Europeans also send their children to the "Army schools" in the province' (RPI-F 1938: 11). By 1946, besides these schools, the following colleges also used English as the medium of instruction, except in the classical and vernacular languages where Urdu was used: Islamia, Edwards, Vedic Bharati, Sanatum Dharan, and the Government College, Abbottabad (RPI-F 1947: 51).

In Sindh, the English schools were mostly in Karachi. By 1939-40, there were three such schools in that city: St Patrick's, St Joseph's, and Jefelhurst. There was one in Hyderabad (St Bonaventure's). The tuition fees in these schools were approximately Rs 99 per year in 1938-9 while the government schools charged Rs 34 during this period. The Progress of Education in India Report for 1932-7 pointed out that there was pressure from the Indian elite to admit more pupils to the English schools than the quota allowed.

The popularity of these schools among Indian parents is thus obviously increasing. This is attributed mainly to a higher standard of instruction and more efficient discipline generally but there is also a tendency on the part of the upper class Indian parents to send their children to these schools with the object of helping them to acquire greater fluency in speaking and writing English (PEI 1939: 236).

The number of Indian pupils in European schools, from the area of present day Pakistan, was as follows in 1938-9.

Table 4.1
Boys

Province	Number of schools	Total number of students	Indians
Punjab	13	1,507	240
NWFP	1	169	67
Sindh	1	281	53
Balochistan	2	241	85
British India	146	24,519	5,590

Table 4.2
Girls

Province	Number of schools	Total number of students	Indians
Punjab	18	1,477	187
NWFP	–	–	–
Sindh	2	299	89
Balochistan	–	–	–
British India	216	28,322	6,286

(Edn Ind 1941: 110)

In 1939, another European school was established in Sindh, which made the figures for 1939-40 as follows: 158 Indians out of a total of 617 (RPI-S 1940: 100).

There was no doubt that these schools were better than the Indian ones. But the 'higher standard of instruction' and 'more efficient discipline' were products of higher investment which the PEI report does not mention, although it does provide figures such as the salaries of teachers and cost per pupil, which lead to that conclusion. The following figures are taken from government reports on education in British India, especially in Sindh and the NWFP, during the 1930s, when Indian schools were being vernacularized.

Table 4.3
Average monthly pay of teachers in schools: (rupees)

Year	Primary	Secondary	European
1932-1937	15-50	40-171	162
1938-1939	20-63	58-186	110-189

Table 4.4
Average cost per pupil per year: (rupees)

Year	Primary	Vernacular	Anglo Vernacular	European
1932-1933	13	22	44	251
1938-1939	14	21	58-107	188

Table 4.5
Average tuition fees per pupil per year: (rupees)

Year	Primary	Vernacular	Anglo Vernacular	European
1932-1933	Free to 2.0	1.4	22-48	75
1939-1940	Free to 1.8	1.4	25-45	87

The high cost of European schooling was justified as follows:

> The cost of European Education is high compared with education in India generally, the cost per pupil in Anglo-Indian and European Institutions being Rs 156 against Rs 14 only in all types of institutions from a university to a primary school. This, however, is not altogether a valid comparison and it is to be noted in this connection that 69 per cent of this cost is met from fees and private donations; in other words public funds bear only 31 per cent of the expenditure (Edn Ind 1941; 113).

Even 31 per cent of the public funds (Rs 48.36) however, was Rs 34 more than the average amount spent on ordinary Indian students. Moreover, ordinary Indians were too poor to be able to afford anything but the free or cheap primary schools. The avowed intention of these schools, as the Indian Education Commission of 1882 announced, was:

The instruction of the masses through the vernacular in such subjects as
will fit them for their position in life, and be not necessarily regarded as a
portion of instruction leading up to the University (Edn Comm 1883:586).

The vernacular secondary schools were also designed to offer a
'complete course,' in contrast to the Anglo-Vernacular schools, which
did teach in English, and could lead up to higher education (PEI 1939:
77). Higher education was expensive—the average yearly fees in the
colleges of Sindh in 1936-7 was Rs 153 and the cost per pupil was
Rs 246 (RPI-S 1938: 21)—so the anglicized elite remained a narrow
aristocracy.

When Pakistan was established, the elitist Mohajir children coming
from English-medium schools in India (out of which thirteen were in
their O' level classes) were admitted in 'the European Schools in
Karachi' (Zaidi 1999: 56). In short, the parallel system of elitist
schooling did not change because of the establishment of Pakistan.
Indeed, as the military and the higher bureaucracy both came from
this elite, these schools multiplied in Pakistan as the professional
middle-class started expanding in the sixties.

Ayub Khan was a Sandhurst-educated officer, who believed in the
superiority of the army over politicians and in the rule of an elite in
the country. He believed that this elite could be created in the English-
medium schools. As the General Officer Commanding in East Pakistan,
he urged the provincial government 'to start good public schools where
intelligent young men' could be trained. With his usual contempt for
politicians and their political constraints, he wrote that Khwaja
Nazimuddin and Nurul Amin:

Seemed to understand what I was talking about but were unwilling or
unable to do anything about it. I never quite understood what they were
afraid of. Perhaps they thought that general reaction to the establishment
of public schools would not be favourable (Khan, A. 1967: 25).

As Commander-in-Chief of the Army, he established 'a number of
cadet colleges and academies' to train those who would one day
administer the country (ibid., 43). As the armed forces encouraged the
use of English even at the cost of all Pakistani languages—in fact the
use of vernaculars was not allowed in the training institutions of the
officer corps—their officers picked up confidence and fluency in the
language. Thus, in a report, which was not made public, the army

reported that the language of its internal use, at least among the officers, would have to remain English.

As we have seen before, the other powerful partner of the army during the Ayub regime, the Civil Service of Pakistan (CSP), was not only traditionally anglicized, like the army, but had a larger number of people from the westernized elite in it. Thus it is no surprise that the government—dominated by members of these two elitist pressure groups—came up with government policies that supported English-medium schools. Let us look at the position two of these reports, the 1958 and the 1966 ones, took regarding these schools.

The Sharif Commission (1958), declared that both Urdu and Bengali would be the medium of instruction from class 6 onwards in the non-elitist schools. While this adversely affected the position of Sindhi, which was the medium of instruction in Sindhi non-elitist schools, as we have seen already, it had no effect on English schools. The policy was defended as follows:

> While we feel that English must yield to the national languages the paramount position that it has occupied in our educational system so far, we are at the same time convinced that English should have a permanent place in the system (GoP, 1959: 288).

The leaders of the Urdu proto-elite criticized this attitude (Abdullah 1976: 59), although most of the criticism against it came from the supporters of the older indigenous languages (see Adil 1962; Ahmad, S. 1968: 3; and editorial of *Mehran*, 31 October 1962 for Sindh).

The Commission on students' problems and welfare, generally called the Hamoodur Rahman Commission (1966), was even more defensive of English than the Sharif commission. Although it was constituted in response to student resistance to some of the recommendations of the Sharif Commission, it went out of its way to criticize the universities that had adopted Urdu as the medium of examination for the BA degree, a popular step with the large majority of students who came from the Urdu-medium schools and had average ability. The Report said:

> We cannot help regretting that some of our universities should have preferred to be swayed more by sentiment than by a dispassionate judgment in accelerating the pace of changeover [to Urdu] beyond all reasonable proportion (GoP, 1966: 114).

The universities singled out were the Karachi University (which had allowed Urdu in 1963), Punjab University (in 1966), and the Sindh University (which had allowed Sindhi, GoP 1966: 114).

During the 1960s, however, there was much criticism of English-medium elitist schools. In 1965, the government reported that it had given grant-in-aid, directly or through local bodies, to a number of such schools. The list provided in the West Pakistan Legislative Assembly consisted of nineteen public schools that were given Rs 2,477,285 in 1964-5, and on whose governing bodies there were seventy-three senior civil and military officers (LAD-WP 5 July 1965: Appendix 111, Question 529). There was some protest against the Lahore Corporation donation of Rs 1,000,000 to the Divisional Public School, whereas the corporation's own schools were in an impecunious condition. However, nothing was done to make amends, and a motion concerning this was disallowed from being even moved in the provincial legislature (LAD-WP 25 January 1965: 67-8).

The Commission, however, defended these schools—the missionary ones on grounds of religious freedom for Christians; and others on the grounds of excellence (GoP 1966: 17-18). Disagreeing with the view that such schools produced snobs, the Commission took the paradoxical plea that they were meant to produce the military and civilian administrative elite. It declared that:

> Such establishments are intended to produce some better type of students who would be more suitably disciplined and equipped for eventually entering the defence service of the country or filling higher administrative posts and other responsible executive positions in the government and semi-government bodies and private firms and corporations (GoP 1966: 18).

The Commission did, however, agree that the existence of such schools violated the constitutional assurance that 'all citizens are equal before law' (Paragraph 15 under Right No. VI), and even recommended that the government 'should not build such schools any more' (GoP 1966: 18). However, it stopped short of making any change in the status quo and recommended that the existing schools be allowed to continue and poor students be given scholarships to study in them (GoP 1966: 18). Thus, despite the criticism leveled by students—such as at the All-Pakistan Students Convention held at Lahore in 1966—against elitist schools (Abdullah 1976: 184), these schools continued to thrive during the Ayub Khan era.

ZIAUL HAQ'S ANTI-ENGLISH SCHOOL POLICY

The most significant anti-English policy of Ziaul Haq was the order that Urdu would be the medium of instruction in all schools from 'class 1 or KG as the case may be from 1979' (PT 4 February 1979). Thus, all students appearing in the matriculation examination in 1989 would use only Urdu. Moreover, the Ministry of Education also said that the nomenclature 'English medium' schools would be abolished (D 18 February 1987). It was reported that several schools did adopt Urdu as the medium of instruction from class 1 and 2 (D 24 November 1980). Visible resistance came from the parents whose children studied in English-medium schools, and who were confronted with a change of language about which they had serious misgivings. Among these were the parents of the Badin PAF Model School (D 6 August 1986) and other parents (MN 15 December 1989 and M 19 April 1984). Some English language dailies also wrote editorials in favor of retaining English in the school system (PT 19 December 1986; N 22 February and 31 August 1987; MN 13 March 1980). The major argument of the English lobby was that Pakistan would fall behind other countries if English were abandoned (Ahmad, S. 1987; Letters to the Editor, MN 5 December 1980; 8 December 1980). To this, the Urdu lobby replied that sufficient books did exist in Urdu and more could be translated. Since parents preferred to teach the language of the domains of power, the Urdu lobby also recommended that all competitive examinations for government service be conducted in Urdu (D 28 December 1981).

However, the elitist schools continued to exist: indeed, they proliferated. By this time, however, most observers felt that the government was not sincere in its policy. An editorial of *The Muslim* (13 May 1987) voiced public opinion by reporting unofficial rumours which suggested that English would be allowed to continue. Naseem Aheer, a minister in the government, stated that Urdu was not fully developed and that the decision to eliminate English had been taken in a hurry (Editorial M 20 May 1987). Syed Sajjad Hyder, the Minister for Education, defended Urdu very strongly (PT 6 October 1987), although a press conference had been held earlier which proposed that the changeover to Urdu, due in 1988, be postponed (NW 13 September 1987; see editorials of PT 16 September 1987 and M 14 September 1987).

The real change in policy occurred in 1983 when Ziaul Haq gave legal protection to the elitist English schools by allowing them to prepare students for the 'O' and 'A' levels examinations of the University of Cambridge through MLR 115 (PT 6 October 1987). On 28 October, the *Pakistan Times* reported:

> The Federal Ministry of Education has decided to continue the existing practice of allowing English as medium of instruction in the science subjects besides Urdu or provincial language in all the secondary schools of the country.

On 11 October, General Ziaul Haq himself allayed the fears of the English lobby by declaring that English could not be abandoned altogether (PT 12 November 1987). According to Lady Viqarunnisa Noon, the General had assured her earlier that she could continue to use English as the medium of instruction in her school. This suggests that the General was under pressure from the westernized elite and that he did not want to alienate them (Noon Int.: 29 December 1994). The reversal of the 1979 education policy, the most momentous step taken in favor of Urdu, was allowed to take place almost silently (see Editorials, N and M 13 November 1987).

THE PRESENT SITUATION

At the moment the federal government has its own English-medium schools. Some of them teach some subjects in English and others in Urdu. The nineteen model colleges of the Federal Government are English-medium schools and colleges. Currently, their enrollment is 30,488 and the cost per student per year is Rs 6,039, much higher than the cost of the Urdu-medium schools of the provincial governments. The military controls eighty-eight Federal English-medium schools in cantonments and garrisons. Moreover, there are elitist public schools under boards of governors such as the Boys Public School and College in Abbottabad and the Sadiq Public School in Bahawalpur as well as cadet colleges and military schools to be dealt with later. Other state-controlled bodies such as the Water and Power Development Authority (WAPDA), the Customs Department, the Pakistan Railways, the Telephone Foundation, and the Police also run English-medium schools. As mentioned earlier, they provide schooling in English, though of varying quality, for affordable fees from their own employees while charging much higher fees from the ordinary public. The armed forces, besides controlling many English-medium schools, also get subsidized education for their dependents from some elitist English-medium schools located in garrisons and cantonments. This means that English-medium schooling can be bought either by the elite of wealth or that of power. And this has not happened through market forces but has been brought about by the functionaries or institutions of the state itself. Indeed, the state has invested heavily in creating a parallel system of education for the elite, especially the elite that would presumably run elitist state institutions in future. This leads to the conclusion that the state does not trust its own system of education and spends public funds to create and maintain the parallel, elitist system of schooling. This strategy of private subversion of publicly stated policies is not peculiar to Pakistan. David D. Laitin, for instance, tells us that in Kazakhstan laws for the learning and use of the Kazakh language were enacted in 1989 but there are 'ardent nationalists who vote to promote 'their' language, yet send their children to more cosmopolitan schools, where the national language is given at best symbolic support' (Laitin 1998: 137). This kind of strategy is observable in all situations where a more empowering language is in clash with a less empowering one. The less empowering one is generally allowed to become the language of the masses while the more empowering one is the preserve of the elite. Such an unjust policy can be reversed but it is generally not. In Pakistan, for instance, it is still in place after more than half a century of the country's existence. The non-elitist system of education, fully dependent upon the state, functions for the most part in Urdu (or in Sindhi and Pashto at places) and gets step-motherly treatment in the allocation of funds, maintenance of buildings, quality of teachers, provision of goods and services, and so on. Most significantly, the non-elitist stream of public education functions in the vernacular rather than in English which means, prima facie, that its products would have greater difficulty in the competition for lucrative and powerful jobs and participation in the elitist domains of power than their English-educated counterparts. More will be said about this later. At the moment let us turn to the public schools/cadet colleges.

Through the Fauji Foundation (Army), Shaheen Foundation (Air Force) and the Bahria Foundation (Navy), the forces created institutions specifically for beneficiaries (retired military personnel) from the 1970s onwards. The Fauji Foundation, for instance, runs eighty-eight secondary and four higher secondary schools. These schools charge low tuition fees from beneficiaries while charging much higher fees from civilians. The rates of tuition fees vary from rural to urban areas and from category to category. In Rawalpindi, for instance, the following rates of fees prevail: retired army non-commissioned ranks pay Rs 150; retired officers, Rs 310; serving non-commissioned ranks, Rs 260; serving officers, Rs 450 while civilians pay Rs 1000 per month for the education of their wards from class 6-10 (information given by the head office of the Fauji Foundation, Rawalpindi). In the army Burn Hall College (Abbottabad) wards of army families pay an average monthly fee of Rs 803 while civilians pay Rs 1458 (the fees is different in all classes but average fees from class 7 to A level has been calculated here). The fee for the boarders is Rs 2956 for those from army families and Rs 3506 for civilians (information from Burn Hall's office). The Air Force says in its manual on the Air University that 'the PAF has come to establish over twenty-five schools and colleges at various bases with an enrollment of over 43,000 students and almost 2000 teachers'. The Military College Jhelum, a cadet college administered by the army, charges Rs 400 per month as tuition fees from armed forces beneficiaries, and Rs 1000 from civilians.

In short, the armed forces have entered the field of English-medium, elitist education and generally provide inexpensive English-medium schooling to their own dependents.

The cadet colleges are subsidized by the state. According to the information given by some of them, the subsidies are as follows:

Table 4.6
Expenditure on Cadet Colleges/Public Schools

Institution	Donation from Provincial Govt.	Number of Students	Yearly cost per student to Govt. (Rs)
Cadet College Kohat	5,819,800	575	10,121
Cadet College Larkana	6,000,000	480	12,500
Cadet College Petaro	14,344,000	700	20,491
Lawrence College	12,000,000	711	16,878
Cadet College Hasanabdal	8,096,000	480	16,867

Source: The offices of the respective institutions have supplied information about donations and number of students.

These subsidies keep changing. In 1998-9 Cadet College Razmak was given Rs 11,887,000 while Larkana got 10,000,000 from the government (*Expenditure* Vol. 1 1999: 1084 and Vol. 2: 1461-1662).

They also receive donations from rich former students, visiting dignitaries and parents of students. In some cases, especially in schools administered by the armed forces, the salaries of officers serving in the schools come from the defence budget. In Military College Jhelum the cadets are given free rations. These too are forms of subsidy which poor children do not receive in the same measure and of the same quality. As one indicator of living conditions, let us look at the area (in acres) available to the students of the best-known cadet colleges/ public schools in Pakistan.

Table 4.7
Area of Cadet Colleges/Public Schools

Institutions	Area in Acres
Aitchison	196
Kohat	144
Larkana	362
Petaro	425
Lawrence	100
Military College	167
Hasanabdal	97
Sadiq Public School	150
Mastung	108

Source: Offices of the respective institutions.

The cadet colleges/public schools are quite expensive—though some are affordable for the middle classes—and their tuition fees increases in senior classes. Since most of their students are boarders, there is also a fee for board and lodging. Then there are other incidental expenses as well as the cost of making European clothes—coat, shirt, trousers, boots, socks, and caps etc.—which make them elitist institutions. The following table gives their budget, average tuition fees (only tuition) and what percent of the budget comes from fees (according to the institution itself) and the cost per student per year.

Table 4.8
Costs of Cadet Colleges/Public Schools

Institution	Budget	Average monthly tuition Fees	Part of the budget covered by fees	Number of students	Total cost per student per year
Aitchison	204,000,000	5,950	80% (163 million)	2120	96,226
Kohat	19,981,217	4,701	44% (8,785,923)	575	34,750
Larkana	23,176,006	550	95% (22,017,205)	480	56,617
Petaro	71,720,000	6000	80% (57,376,000)	700	1,02,457
Lawrence	98,886,181	2000	18.19% (17,987,396)	711	1,39,080
Hasanabdal	48,223,000	1350	12.75% (6,148,433)	480	100,465
Mastung	36,300,000	2200	15.75% (5,500,000)	360	100,834

Source: Offices of the respective institutions except for the cost per student per year, which was obtained by dividing the total budget by the number of students. For details see Annexure 5.

Thus, while cadet colleges have excellent boarding and lodging arrangements, spacious playgrounds, well equipped libraries, laboratories and faculty with masters' degrees, the ordinary Urdu-medium (and Sindhi-medium) schools sometimes do not even have benches for pupils to sit on. In short, contrary to its stated policy of spending public funds on giving the same type of schooling to all, the state (and its institutions) actually spend more funds on privileged children for a privileged (English-medium) form of schooling. This perpetuates the socio-economic inequalities which have always existed in Pakistani society.

The textbooks of Cadet College are in English but these are mostly from the Textbook Boards. Their teachers, generally from the middle classes, also expose them to anti-India, pro-military ideas. Moreover, as most students are boarders they are not exposed to cable TV as their elitist school counterparts are.

Boys in the cadet colleges belong to middle class backgrounds (56.90 per cent—see Annexure 1 for details).

They are used to some regimentation in their schools. Like the students of other English-medium schools, they are also supportive of less militant and less intolerant policies than their counterparts in the madrassas. However, possibly because of regimentation and closeness to the military in some cases, they are somewhat more aggressive and intolerant towards the religious minorities and women than the students of elitist English-medium schools.

Table 4.9
Militancy Among Cadet College/Public Schools
(N=130) (%)

What should be Pakistan's priorities?	Yes	No	Don't Know
1. Take Kashmir away from India by an open war?	36.92	60.00	3.08
2. Take Kashmir away from India by supporting Jihadi groups to fight with the Indian army?	53.08	40.00	6.92
3. Support Kashmir cause through peaceful means only (i.e. no open war or sending Jihadi groups across the line of control)	56.15	36.92	6.92

Source: Survey 2003 (Annexure 2).

They are also less tolerant towards religious minorities than their counterparts in the elitist English-medium schools as the figures below illustrate:

Table 4.10
Tolerance Among Cadet Colleges/Public Schools 2003
(N=130) (%)

What should be Pakistan's priorities?

	Yes	No	Don't Know
1. Give equal rights to Ahmedis in all jobs etc?	41.54	36.92	21.54
2. Give equal rights to Pakistani Hindus in all jobs etc?	64.62	31.54	3.85
3. Give equal rights to Pakistani Christians in all jobs etc?	76.92	18.46	4.62
4. Give equal rights to men and women as in Western countries?	67.69	25.38	6.92

Source: Annexure 2.

Students of these schools are as alienated from the peoples' culture and aspirations as other elitist children. Like them, they too desire to preserve and perpetuate their privileged position by supporting English as the language of the domains of power in the country (see survey 2000 in Rahman 2002: Appendix 14.3).

The teachers of these schools are generally (56 per cent) male from the middle classes (see Annexure 1 for details). They appear to be supportive of peace rather than war as the following figures indicate:

Table 4.11
Militancy Among Cadet College/Public School Teachers
(N=51) (%)

	Yes	No	Don't Know
1. Open War	19.61	68.63	11.76
2. Jihadi Groups	39.22	52.94	7.84
3. Peaceful means	66.66	19.61	13.73

Source: Annexure 2.

They are tolerant of Hindus and Christians but not of Ahmedis and women as for as equality of rights is concerned:

Table 4.12
Tolerance of Religious Minorities and Women in Cadet College/
Public School Teachers—2003
(N=51) (%)

		Yes	No	Don't Know
(1)	Ahmedis	29.41	62.75	7.84
(2)	Hindus	60.78	35.29	3.92
(3)	Christians	60.78	33.33	5.88
(4)	Women	37.25	58.82	3.92

Source: Annexure 2.

These figures should be taken with a note of caution because the sample of fifty-one teachers is rather small. Moreover, in some schools military officers also teach the boys but such schools were not part of this sample.

ELITIST ENGLISH-MEDIUM SCHOOLS

Apart from the schools run by agencies of the state itself—the federal government, the armed forces, the bureaucracy—in contravention of the stated policy of providing vernacular-medium education at state expense, there are private schools, which deal in selling English at exorbitant prices. Private schools catering to the elite have existed since British times as we have seen earlier. In Pakistan the convents were such types of schools and most Anglicized senior members of the elite are from institutions that were called Jesus and Mary's Convent (Lahore and Karachi); Saint Anthony's (Lahore); Burn Hall (Abbottabad); Saint Mary's (Rawalpindi); St. Joseph's Convent (Karachi); Presentation Convent (Rawalpindi) and convents in Murree and other places. These schools were not as expensive as those that replaced them from 1985 onwards. The new schools, which took their place were Beaconhouse, City School, Froebels, Roots, Grammar

(Lahore) and Khaldunia. Most of them have campuses spread all over
the country though all are not of equal quality. They charge tuition
fees of Rs 1500 and more per month and prepare students for the
British Ordinary and Advanced level examinations. Their faculty,
especially at the senior levels, is paid better than government school
teachers (Rs 10,000 per month plus). However, there are vast
differences in salaries even in the same school and full data on salaries
is not released. On the whole, women from the middle classes, some
of who are themselves from English-medium schools, are employed
as teachers. Male teachers, however, tend to be from lower socio-
economic backgrounds.

The teaching methods in these institutions are more humane,
modern, innovative and interesting than in the Urdu-medium schools
and the madrassas. Books are printed abroad and have pictures and
more general knowledge than found in Textbook Board textbooks.
The classics of English, generally in abridged forms, are used to teach
English. World history is taught instead of the propagandist form of
Pakistan studies. However, the O' level examination makes the study
of Pakistan studies, Islamic studies and Urdu compulsory even for
these children.

Since textbooks contain perspectives from various parts of the world
(in English medium schools), and such students have access to cable
TV, literature from the West, and interact with adults who are versed
in a variety of discourses, children from English medium schools learn
to be more tolerant of the 'other.' They are tolerant of people from
different religions (such as Hinduism) and of different countries (such
as India). These children are much less supportive of militant policies
in Kashmir than their counterparts in other schools.

The present survey has been conducted with [116] students,
63 males and 53 females, of the average age of 15 who are in class-10
(O' level) in schools of Islamabad and Lahore charging tuition fees of
at least Rs 2,500 per month. Most of them belong to the upper-middle
and the upper classes (see Annexure 1 for details).

Besides what the students have written, an indicator of their socio-
economic background is the exorbitant tuition fee their parents pay;
their dress (Western and expensive); their lifestyle (travelling in cars,
eating out, going to concerts, celebrating birthdays with parties and
expensive gifts etc.), and the houses they live in (modern, expensive,
urban). They do not support militant policies as the following figures
indicate:

Table 4.13
Militancy Among Elitist English-medium School Students
(N=116) (%)

What should be Pakistan's priorities?

	Yes	No	Don't Know
1. Take Kashmir away from India by an open war?	25.86	64.66	9.48
2. Take Kashmir away from India by supporting Jihadi group to fight with theIndian army?	22.41	60.34	17.24
3. Support Kashmir cause through peaceful means only (i.e. no open war or sending Jihadi groups are on the line of Control)	72.41	18.97	8.62

Source: Annexure 2. Figures do not add up correctly because some students ticked 'Yes' for questions 1 and/or 2 as well as 'Yes' to 3, which is contradictory.

They are also more tolerant of religious minorities and more supportive of giving equal rights to women than their counterparts in the Urdu-medium schools and the madrassas.

Table 4.14
Tolerance Among Elitist English-medium School Students
(N=116) (%)

What should be Pakistan's priorities?

	Yes	No	Don't Know
1. Gives equal rights to Ahmedis in all jobs etc?	65.52	9.48	25.00
2. Give equal rights to Pakistani Hindus in all jobs?	78.45	13.79	7.76
3. Give equal right to Pakistani Christians in all jobs etc?	83.62	8.62	7.76
4. Given equal rights to men and women as in Western countries?	90.52	6.03	3.45

Source: Annexure 2.

The teachers of these schools, who happen to be mostly women, are also supportive of a peaceful foreign policy but are not as tolerant of religious minorities as their students.

Table 4.15
Militancy and Tolerance Among Elitist
English-medium School Teachers
N= 65 (Number = No.)(F= 47; M=18) (%)

Abbreviated Questions		Yes	No	Don't Know
(1)	Open War	26.15	64.62	9.23
(2)	Jihadi Groups	38.46	50.77	10.77
(3)	Peaceful means	60.00	33.85	6.15
(4)	Ahmedis	43.07	36.92	20.00
(5)	Hindus	61.54	26.15	12.31
(6)	Christians	81.54	10.77	7.69
(7)	Women	78.46	13.85	7.69

NB: Figures for (3) are un-interpretable because some respondents ticked opinion (1) and/or (2) while also ticking (3). For details see Annexure 2.

One explanation for this observation—of teachers being less tolerant than their students—is that the teachers belong to middle-class socio-economic backgrounds (see Annexure 1 for details) whereas the students belong to more affluent and Westernized ones.

Another indicator of teachers having climbed up the socio-economic ladder is that whereas 21.28 per cent said they were educated in Urdu-medium schools themselves, only 3.70 per cent have children studying in these schools now (the non-response to the question about own medium of instruction in school is 27.69 per cent and for children's medium of instruction is 58.46 per cent). By talking to the teachers, however, it becomes clear that they were either educated in non-elitist (so-called) English-medium schools or, perhaps, claim to have been educated in them because they feel ashamed to confess that they were not.

CAREER PROSPECTS OF ENGLISH-MEDIUM STUDENTS

Graduates of English schools either join multinational corporations within the country or go to join the international bureaucracy from where they often drift back home to fashionable NGOs and foreign banks. Not as many join either the civil bureaucracy or the officer corps of the armed forces as before (in the 50s and 60s). Those who do appear in the armed forces and civil service competitive examinations do better than their vernacular-educated counterparts. As the armed forces release no figures, one can only conjecture through personal observation that those who are most fluent in English are at a great advantage in their career. For the bureaucracy, however, figures are available to confirm that products of English schools stand a better chance of passing in the public service examination.

Table 4.16
Results of Civil Services Examinations Expressed in Percentage

	Year	Appeared %	Passes %
Vernacular-medium (including pseudo-English-medium)	1996	78	65
	1997	75	67
	1998	67	58
English-medium	1996	3	11.5
	1997	21	34
	1998	20	31

Source: Annual Reports of the Federal Public Service Commission of Pakistan 1996, 1997, 1998, Islamabad: Federal Public Service Commission, 1999.

Those classified here as pseudo-English-medium institutions are not given as such in the reports. These are such Federal Government and private schools that claim to be English-medium. These are included among the vernacular-medium schools because their students are only marginally more competent in English than the students of vernacular-medium schools.

PRIVATE NON-ELITIST SCHOOLS

By far the largest number of the so-called English-medium schools is English-medium only in name. According to a 1987 survey of Rawalpindi-Islamabad, there were sixty English-medium schools in Islamabad and 250 in Rawalpindi. Out of these 250 only thirty-nine were recognized schools (Awan 1987). In the matriculation examinations of 1999, a total of 119,673 candidates appeared from the Board of Intermediate and Secondary Education, Lahore. Out of these, according to the records in the Board office, 6923 (5.8 per cent) were from English-medium schools. Most of these candidates (6448) were from the city itself. The recent survey conducted by the government has shown a total of 33,893 institutions of general education in the private sector. Though the medium of instruction is not given most of them profess to be English-medium schools (Census Private 2001: 12). And, indeed, one can see such schools concentrated in the cities though they are fast appearing even in small towns now all over the country. Their fees ranges between Rs 50 to Rs 1500 per month, which is far higher than the average state vernacular school but lower than that of the elitist private English school. In these schools pretence is made of teaching most subjects in English. In general teachers write answers of all subjects on the board, which students faithfully copy, memorize and reproduce in the examination.

The Principal of the Federal Government Girls High Secondary Model School in Islamabad said that her school was only a 'so-called' English school. Only mathematics and science subjects were taught in English while all the other subjects were taught in Urdu. And yet, so high is the demand for English, that there are about 3000 students, half of whom attend the evening classes (Naqvi Int. 1999).

The Federal Government Model schools, cadet colleges, elitist public schools, and armed forces schools do, however, teach English at a higher standard than the vernacular-medium schools. The public schools, mindful of their elitist reputation, try to supplement the prescribed Textbook Board books with others. From IX, however, they adhere to the prescribed syllabi that are meant to promote Pakistani nationalism as has been mentioned earlier and will be touched upon again.

Recently, chains of non-elitist English-medium schools run by organized bodies have sprung up in Pakistan. One such organization is Language Enhancement and Achievement Program (LEAP) run by the

Aga Khan Education Service in the Northern Areas and Chitral. LEAP courses 'attempt to impart teacher-specific language and to improve teachers' command of classroom language'. The teachers are taught English for three months in courses. The programme started in May 1996 and focused on D.H. Howe's *Active English*, which is taught in English-medium schools in Pakistan. In 1997 the programme was also extended to Chitral. It was expected to train eighty-eight teachers in Chitral and 132 in the Northern Areas by the end of 1997. By the end of 1997 there were over twenty English-medium schools in the Gilgit and Ghizer districts, which sent their teachers to the LEAP courses. In short, LEAP is increasing competence in English at the school level in a hitherto neglected area of Pakistan (this information is taken from LEAP 1997 & field research).

Another chain of schools goes by the name of Hira English-medium schools. The Hira Educational Project created this chain in 1990 in Lahore. In 1997 the name was change to Hira National Educational Foundation. The aim of this project is to educate students along both Islamic and modern lines. Thus the Arabic language and Islamic moral lessons are taught from class I but the books of science and mathematics are in English. Social studies is taught in Urdu and Urdu is compulsory. Since the children are from modest backgrounds, as are the teachers, interaction is generally in Urdu or the local language. At present there are thirteen regions in which these schools operate. The total number of institutions is 215 including four colleges. About 45,000 students are enrolled in these institutions (Hira Central Directorate 2003 in Ahmed 2003). The author found class I children mostly speaking in Kalam Kohistani in Hira School Matiltan, nine kilometers from Kalam (Swat), though the teachers spoke to them in Urdu (Nabi Int. 1998).

Yet another chain of the Islamic schools, both Urdu- and English-medium, is the Siqara school system. A girls' school in a lower-middle-class locality in Lahore makes both students and teachers wear the *hijab* (scarf covering the head and bosom) while books are checked for their anti-Islamic content. Indeed, the principal of one of the boy's schools of the Siqara system told me that he had changed the pictures of women by drawing full sleeves and head scarves by his own pen in English books for use in their schools.

It seems that the Islamic revivalist thinkers have realized how empowering English is and want to attract lower income groups through it. Thus, Khalid Ahmed has a point when he says that '90 per cent' of the English-medium institutions—not only schools, of course—are middle-class 'Islamist institutions' (Ahmed 1999: 5). While the percentage may be contested, there is no doubt that Islamists, especially those who are politically oriented, teach English because it enables students to enter the mainstream for positions of power in the salariat. This policy has also been endorsed by the Jamaat-i-Islami which, while being against English-medium elitist schools, does not deny either secular education or English to the students who study in its institutions.

Yet another experiment on-going in the North-West Frontier Province is where the children of the industrial workers are given English-medium education in schools that are cleaner and better maintained than government Urdu-medium schools. Their teachers also claim to function in English and, judging by the qualifications of some of them, may be doing so. As yet eight such schools have been established in different cities of the NWFP. They have 4,388 students and their cost per student per year is Rs 7,138. But this includes free textbooks, free transport and even free uniform for the children of the workers. The tuition fee is Rs 30 per month for industrial workers but other children are charged higher fees (Hasan Int. 2003 and information from the office of the Directorate of Education, NWFP). On the whole, for the cost, the workers' children have a better deal under the circumstances than they would get anywhere else.

PRODUCTS OF NON-ELITIST ENGLISH SCHOOLS

The graduates of these schools are, in any case, less Westernized that those of the elitist English schools—especially schools with students from Westernized families. They are also not as fluent in English as the students of missionary schools used to be and the private elitist schools are even now. In Senior Army Burn Hall, where was a student between 1960-5, students used to speak English with each other and with the teachers. Now, however, they do not. The principal, however, said that he still used English with the students (Arshad Int. 1997). This is more or less the situation in other similar schools.

It seems to me that the idea behind the non-elitist English schools is good, but is nevertheless, deceptive and illusory. People want their children to learn English because it is the language of power and prestige. But calling a school English-medium does not make it cross the class boundaries, which go by the name of English. One learns to operate in a certain manner and speak English spontaneously through interaction with the peer group and family rather than teachers who themselves cannot operate in English naturally. This is where the illusion comes in. The parents spend so much money, which they can ill afford, chasing the elusive chimera of English. These are dreams and these schools sell dreams. This, by itself, would be wrong but what makes it worse is that people, deluded by the seemingly easy availability of English, make no effort to change this system of educational apartheid.

Even up to class IX, the students of state-influenced English schools are exposed to the Pakistani worldview through texts, interaction with teachers, family and peers. From class IX onwards all the books they study are prescribed by Textbook Boards. They do study subjects in English—in some schools, however, Pakistan Studies is in Urdu—but their books are saturated with state-sponsored ideology.

The main Urdu textbook is *Muraqqa-e-Urdu*, which has a number of essays on Islamic personalities, historical personages from the Pakistan movement, and war heroes. There is a slim section on poetry but amorous verse—which constitutes the best *ghazals*—is conspicuous by its absence. The English texts are of a similar kind. Apart from the usual essays on the historical personalities there are essays on the low intensity conflict going on between India and Pakistan on the Siachen glacier, the highest battlefield in the world. This war is represented as a triumph of heroism. In short, the ideological content of English texts is not much different from those in Urdu. There may, however, be some difference in the way different teachers indoctrinate their students. The common perception of a large number of students and teachers is that the teachers of Urdu are more orthodox, supportive of middle-class, Islamic, and nationalist values than teachers of English. The teachers' values and attitudes, however, generally reflect his or her class background, socialization, education, and personality. Since puritanical Islam, chauvinism, and militarism are supported by the middle-classes, especially the educated lower middle class, teachers from this background tend to incorporate their class world view into their teaching.

CURRICULA OF ELITIST ENGLISH-MEDIUM SCHOOLS

The curricula of the elitist English-medium schools and the other English-medium schools are different. Let us first take the curricula of elitist schools like Beaconhouse, City School, Froebels, etc. The books on English and Urdu—the only languages taught in these schools— are generally not of the Pakistan Textbook Board till class IX which then are used only if the student wants to appear in the Pakistani matriculation (class X) examination. Some schools, like Froebels, do not even permit their students to appear in the matriculation examination. All students take the British ordinary and advanced level school certificate examinations. Thus, most students study books originally written for Western school children. Some books have been especially reprinted for Pakistan but the changes made in them are minor—the clothes of women are Pakistani and characters sometimes have Pakistani names—while other books are still meant for a Western readership. These texts socialize a child into English-speaking Western culture. Children read classics such as *Lorna Doone*, *Little Women*, *Wuthering Heights*, and *Tom Brown's School Days* and famous figures like Florence Nightingale and so on. The world portrayed here is Western, middle-class, and successful. It is a secular world of nuclear families where women generally perform the household chores though they are sometimes seen as doing other work too. The overwhelming message of the texts is liberal and secular. Concepts like the segregation or veiling of women, ubiquitous religiosity, sectarianism or ethnicity get no support.

Even the Urdu textbooks, as mentioned in the previous chapter, are published by private publishers and are less supportive of state ideology than those of the Textbook Boards. However, all Pakistani children have to study Urdu, Pakistan Studies, and Islamic Studies, which expose them to official state ideology in varying degrees. In the 1950s and the early 60s elitist English-medium school children did not study such subjects at all and may have been more Westernized than even elitist children are today.

As for the schools in the third, as it were lumpen category, they are more or less close to the vernacular-medium schools than the English schools which they claim to be. This is because their fee structure and lack of facilities attract students from socio-economic backgrounds where English is hardly used. Similarly, their salary structure only attracts teachers who are not fluent—indeed not even tolerably competent—in English at all. Curricula and examinations are in English. However, they are only one aspect of teaching English. The other aspect is the quality of teaching and the third, and most important, is the frequency of informal interaction with English speaking people. Formal training of teachers appears to me to be far less important than their command of the language. The salaries of schools, even of elitist schools, are not attractive enough for men from elitist English-using backgrounds. Women, especially women from affluent families, are, however, attracted by these salaries because they do not have to support the whole family only on their income. If these women are from English-using backgrounds, they speak to their students both within the classroom and outside it in a natural manner in English. This provides the students the key component of interaction with English-using people—something which less Anglicized schools lack.

But even more important than the teachers are students' playmates and members of the family as far as informal interaction is concerned. If they are from English speaking backgrounds the child gets exposure to English not only in the classroom but also outside it. Indeed, it is this exposure which makes the crucial difference between a child from a good English-medium school and a mediocre one. The former learns to interact in English in an informal way, a point I mentioned earlier in the context of the alleged snobbery of English-school students. It bears repetition that the spoken English of elitist school graduates is spontaneous and is pronounced differently from the English of other Pakistanis (I have described this in my book *Pakistani English* [Rahman 1990] earlier).

This fluency and spontaneity in the use of English is not so much a product of courses of study, techniques of teaching, and examinations. It is, above all, a product of exposure to English in the informal domain. But this exposure cannot be provided in the school alone no matter how hard the teachers work and whichever books are prescribed. It is, in the last analysis, a byproduct of power—of Anglicization, which is the preserve of powerful and affluent people. They use English at home and their children are exposed to it even before joining school. Women from these families, educated in elitist English schools themselves, become English speaking teachers and provide role models for their pupils. The whole atmosphere of school, playground, and home is English speaking. Even the leisure hours of the children expose them to English. They watch English cartoons; read English comic books; English children's fiction, English popular fiction, and are constantly exposed to CNN, BBC and television programmes in English. Thus, children in rich and expensive English schools, but not in English schools in less affluent or less Anglicized areas, become fluent and spontaneous in English. In short, command over English is related to power and its corollaries—Anglicization of culture, possession of wealth, and so on. Thus, command over English is highest in the elitist schools followed by the state-influenced English schools, the non-elitist English schools and is least in the vernacular-medium schools.

CONCLUSION

The children of English schools can be roughly divided into two kinds: the products of the elitist private schools, especially those who have a large majority of children from Westernized elitist homes, and those of the state-influenced schools. There are, of course, varying shades between these broad categories nor is any category definable in a precise way. Very roughly, then, the former are more Westernized than other Pakistani children. The negative consequence of this is that they are alienated from Pakistan, especially from its indigenous languages and cultures. This makes some of them look down upon most things indigenous. While such people are neither aware nor in sympathy with the values, feelings and aspirations of their countrymen or women, they are generally believers in liberal-humanist and democratic values. Thus they are less susceptible to sectarian prejudices or the persecution of Hindus, Ahmedis and non-Muslims in Pakistan. Less exposed to nationalistic and militaristic propagand, they are also less prone to India-bashing and undue glorification of war and the military. The products of the state-influenced English schools have more in common with middle-class urban Pakistanis than the ones we have just described. However, like them, they too are alienated from villagers and have little understanding of the indigenous cultures of the country. They are not susceptible to sectarian prejudices but, being nationalistic and militaristic, they are quite anti-India and supportive of the military.

As we can see in the chart given in Rahman (2002: Appendix 14) the students of the ordinary English-medium schools are similar in their responses to those of Urdu-medium ones. The views of these students have not been ascertained in the present survey of 2003 precisely for this reason. However, the views of other students, including those from Urdu and English medium schools, were obtained and have been discussed earlier and shown in the annexures. The students of the elitist English-medium schools are notably less prone to an aggressive policy on Kashmir and are most liberal towards Ahmedis.

All products of English schools, even those who are English-medium only in name, agree in regarding themselves as an elite—not of money and power, which they are, but of talent and knowledge. They hold the products of the government vernacular-medium schools in open contempt. Indeed, to be 'Urdu-medium' or *paendoo* [rustic], is a term of derision among them. They are alienated from their society whose values they hold in contempt. While there is no doubt that some of these values, such as that of the honour killing of women for suspected sexual transgressions, are abominable and should be opposed, it does not mean that everything about Pakistani society is to be condemned. What is worse is that it is not only certain values or customs, which these 'foreigners' living in Pakistan dismiss derisively; they hold all Pakistanis, except Westernized ones, in contempt. They are what people call 'brown Englishmen' (Vittachi 1987). This kind of dismissal of everything 'native' is one of the worst legacies of colonial, Western rule. It was also common in South Africa as none other than the man who contributed to the decolonization of the African mind, Nelson Mandela, says about his boyhood:

The educated Englishman was our model. What we aspired to were "black Englishmen", as we were sometimes derisively called. We were taught—and believed—that the best ideas were English ideas, the best government was English government, and the best men were Englishmen (Mandela 1994: 32).

This was the condition in my own school in the 1960s and is still the condition in elitist English-medium schools today. What has changed, however, is that whereas English culture was the model in the sixties, the present model comes from the United States. One's own countrymen and women are looked down upon just as they were by the Western colonizers. The English schools, then, produce snobs with only one redeeming feature—some of these snobs, because of their liberal-humanist values, support human rights, democracy and freedom. However, even this support is very often confined only to the young and the idealistic. After all, those products of these schools who become functionaries of the state are the ones who create both the policies and their rationalization which disempower and further pauperize the poor. And whatever they may believe in private, or profess to believe in fashionable company, they do not do anything to change laws that discriminate against religious minorities and women. So, on the whole, the English-medium schools do not redeem themselves by any but the most superficial and snobbish criteria of judgement.

The Author's Story

On both sides of the road going from Abbottabad to Manshera were huge trees and the green foliage almost came up to the edge of the narrow road. There were a few houses near a place known as Supply and then only scattered mud houses and trees. Suddenly, after a small petrol station, a huge red building stood poised against the whale-like green but treeless mountains. There were huge playing fields in front of the building and a canal flowed right in the centre of the grounds. This was Senior Burn Hall, a school run by European Roman Catholic missionaries. In 1948 it had been moved from Srinagar to Abbottabad and was known as one of the best English-medium convent schools in Pakistan.

It was the spring of 1960 when I entered this imposing building with shining terrazzo floors and cheerful classrooms with yellow glass windows. The next five years were among the best in my life. Father Scanlon was the headmaster and he did not style himself as 'principal' as almost every head of an English-medium school does nowadays. Father Doyle, a good-natured Irishman, looked after the stationery shop. Another priest collected our fees and the irrepressible Father Johnson, probably the most colourful priest in the history of the school, looked after the huge grounds with the pond, the canal, the orchards and the swimming pools. There were no clerks, no PAs, no deputy heads, no bursars, no administrative officers—no nothing! There were, of course, gardeners, cooks, waiters, one driver and one peon. And, how could I forget them, there were two PT masters who saw to it that boys would not remain idle.

Life was easygoing and the priests were generally not tyrants. We played with marbles right before their eyes. We caught their fish. We stole the unripe plums and apples. Boys would be boys and they did not steal away our boyhood from us. Nor were we overburdened with too much homework or taxed with too many extra curricular activities.

We were exposed to English in various ways. First, a European priest always taught English. Some, like Father Doyle, taught it in a dry but proficient manner making us learn grammar and write essays. Others had a laissez faire style telling us stories and making us recite poetry. And Father Johnson was in a class all by himself. He had a huge vocabulary of words that he would write on the board. He also read out English novels filling us up on the history of English literature. He always sat on top of his desk resting his sandaled feet—yes, he wore Peshawar-style *chappals*—on one of the chairs in front of him. We learned much from him and others who read out stories. It gave us a vast vocabulary, familiarized us with the pronunciation of English and kindled our imagination.

I do not think the regimented English-medium schools of today would ever tolerate such teachers. In these schools, much to my horror, the principal can enter any class much to the humiliation of the teacher—

something that never happened in my school. The teachers maintain all kinds of planners, diaries and other instruments of regimentation curbing their independence and making them prisoners of the administration. They cannot even sit down in the classroom if they want to—such are the impositions of the new age.

We also learned English from peers. Most boys spoke with each other in English even informally. The number of European boys was very small, indeed, but that is how we Pakistanis spoke with each other. We also read comic books, that were, of course, in English. Some of us, myself included, read the classics of English literature borrowing them every Saturday from the school library.

The school did not force students to appear for the final matriculation or O' level examination in less than the time given for it. Nor did we start preparing for the final year examinations in junior classes. We received the whole experience of education in a slow, gentle, unhurried manner. But now, during the course of my research, I came across schools that had begun teaching final year books in the 8th class and some that had forced students to take the O' level examination in two rather than the stipulated three years.

With all the fun we had, we knew that if we did not apply ourselves to studies we would fail. Most of us did so and the number of failures was very small. Then we entered the world of the college and came across Urdu-medium schoolboys. We had only seen them filing out of their schools in gray *shalwar qameez* with *taktis* (wooden slates) in their hands. We thought they were too distant from our lives, and knew little about them. Most of us prided ourselves on not knowing Urdu very well. And Urdu literature was a taboo; it tended to compromise one's status as an English-school boy. In short, most of us were snobs but we generally did not know that.

But slowly, those who could not join elitist social circles, started getting 'nativized'. They picked up fluent Punjabi and developed the habit of carrying on conversations in Punjabi, Urdu and a few phrases of English thrown in here and there rather than in the reverse order. This started off as a tactic—only a way of joining the majority group—but it became a habit. Those who found their way into elitist circles did not have to change themselves and English remained their badge of identity.

Very few, like myself, realized the injustice of this educational apartheid. I wanted to do away with such elitist schools. But I knew that I could not afford not to teach my own children in them because not to learn English would be to weaken one's self. One can fight against injustice from a position of strength not weakness. So I sent them to the same kind of schools. The dilemma now is whether they would remain alienated from their society and snobs at that or whether they would use their skills to understand, expose and change this apartheid system of schooling.

The Peripatetic Tutor

Arif Khan (not his real name) had done his M.Sc. in mathematics and it was years after that he landed a job in a famous elitist English-medium school. Most of his colleagues were women because men went for more lucrative jobs than school teaching. Many of them were from rich families and had studied in similar schools because they spoke in English even with each other. The students, both girls and boys, also spoke in English with each other and he had a difficult time just sticking out the mathematics period.

But one day a boy approached him for tuition. He had heard of such things happening and readily consented. He had to go to the boy's house, a huge palace as far as he could make out, with two cars in the driveway and a ferocious dog that barked like mad. But they were decent people and paid well. The boy did his O' levels with an 'A' in mathematics and next year he had to tutor four boys. This time he got A' level students and had to stay up nights to learn their books before he taught them. But again they all got 'A' grades and this time he could no longer teach all who wanted to study because by the time he reached home it was always midnight.

In four years, he had a car and had resigned from the school. He now taught in four elitist schools driving fast from one to the other all day long. In the evening he had his own academy and twenty students attended in one shift. In the second shift, which went on till past ten in the night, there were another fifteen.

Each of the students paid Rs 3000 and then there was the income from the four schools. He was earning nearly two *lacs* (200,000) rupees per month and not even paying a tax except on income from one school.

He had built a house and both he and his wife had their own cars. The three children went to the most expensive schools in the city. But his life was one of running from school to school and then to his academy to teach, teach and teach till his feet ached and he was ready to drop. He had no friends because he had no time for anyone. He read nothing on any subject, not even the newspaper, because his peripatetic existence did not allow him that luxury. He did, however, keep in touch with the O' and A' level syllabi and any new course books that had recently come from Britain. That was his livelihood, but beyond that he knew nothing though in his university days he had played with the idea of becoming a great mathematician. That dream was buried forever now.

But he did not know he would have to bury the dream of the family. He learned when he found that the children he had given no time and no attention to hardly knew him. Indeed, they resented him—resented him even when he had bought them all the computers, all the video games, all the gadgets they asked for. Both the boys had been thrown out of every institution he sent them to till he had sent them to America where he had paid thousands of dollars for fake MBA degrees. The girl had done well but the man who married her, it turned out, wanted a house in his name. He did all that his children demanded. He now looked forward to retirement and ease at last.

One day, when all these bills had been paid, he found that he had no savings for his old age. He was so tired; so burnt-out; so very weary with it all that he wanted to give up—to disappear; to go back to the small house in the crowded street he spent his childhood in. This house where his wife lived was a palace. But he hardly lived here. Indeed, he lived in the car and the classroom. Couldn't he just sit in the house doing nothing—just watching TV and reading books and talking to his wife as people did? No! He knew he could not. He had to do his tuitions and schools again because that and that alone was his life insurance. It was the only pension he would ever have.

5

MADRASSAS

The madrassas have been in the news a great deal after 9/11 and are perceived to be the breeding ground for the Taliban, who were students of these institutions and subsequently rose to power in Afghanistan in the mid-90s (see Rashid 2000). Madrassas have also been much in the news for alleged involvement in sectarian killings and supporting militancy in Kashmir. They are considered breeding grounds of the Jihadi culture—a term used for Islamic militancy in the English-language press of Pakistan (Singer 2001; Haqqani 2002; Ahmad 2000: 191-192).

There was not much writing on the madrassas before the events of 9/11 in Pakistan. J.D. Kraan, writing for the Christian Study Centre, had provided a brief introduction (Kraan 1984). Later, A.H. Nayyar, an academic, updated this introduction arguing that sectarian violence was traceable to madrassa education (Nayyar 1998). Both used only secondary sources. Later, I wrote on language teaching in the madrassas (Rahman 2002). The book also contained a survey of the opinions of madrassa students on Kashmir, the implementation of the *Sharia*, equal rights for religious minorities and women, freedom of the media, democracy (Rahman 2002: Appendix 14). The seminal work on the *ulema*, and the madrassas in which they are trained, is by Qasim Zaman (2002). This is an excellent study of how the traditional ulema can be differentiated from the Islamists who react to modernity by attempting to go back to fundamentalist, and essentially political, interpretations of Islam.

The *ulema* or the Islamists in Pakistan write, generally in Urdu, in defence of the madrassas, that the state sought to modernize and secularize. Two recent books, a survey by the Institute of Policy Studies (patronized by the revivalist, Islamist, Jamaat-i-Islami) of the madrassas (IPS 2002) and a longer book by Saleem Mansur Khalid (Khalid 2002), are useful because they contain much recent data.

Otherwise the work of the Pakistani *ulema* is polemical and tendentious. They feel themselves increasingly besieged by Western (Singer 2001) and Pakistani secular critics (Haqqani 2002; Ahmad 2000: 191-192) and feel that they should defend their position from the inside rather than wait for sympathetic outsiders to do it for them (as defended by Sikand 2001)

There is very little credible information on the unregistered madrassas. However, those that are registered are controlled by their own central organizations or boards. These organizations determine the syllabi, collect a registration fees and an examination fees. They set and distribute the examination papers, in Urdu and Arabic, to the madrassas where pupils take their examinations. They also compile and declare the results. The names of the boards are as follows:

Table 5.1
Central Boards of Madrassas in Pakistan

Name	Sub-Sect	Location	Date Established
Wafaq ul Madaris	Deobandi	Multan	1959
Tanzim ul Madaris	Barelvi	Lahore	1960
Wafaq ul Madaris (Shia) Pakistan	Shia	Lahore	1959
Rabta-tul-Madaris-al-Islamia	Jamat-i-Islami	Lahore	1983
Wafq-ul-Madaris-al-Salafia	Ahl-i-Hadith	Faislabad	1955

Source: Offices of the respective Boards.

At independence, there were about 137 madrassas. In April 2002, Dr Mahmood Ahmed Ghazi, the Minister of Religious Affairs, put the figure at 10,000 with 1.7 million students (ICG 2002: 2). These institutions belong to the major sects of Islam, the Sunnis and the Shias. However, Pakistan being a predominantly Sunni country, Shia run madrassas are very few. Among those run by Sunnis there are three sub-sects: Deobandis, Barelvis and the Ahl-i-Hadith (*salafi*). Besides these, the revivalist Jamaat-e-Islami also has its own madrassas.

The number of madrassas has increased since General Ziaul Haq's rule (1977-1988). During the war by Islamic Afghan groups in Afghanistan against the Soviet Union the United States sent in money, arms and ammunition through Pakistan which is said to have been used to support the madrassas. Later, presumably because religiously inspired and madrassa students infiltrated across the line of control to fight the Indian army in Kashmir, they were supported by the Pakistan army (specifically the Inter Services Intelligence agency). However, both the ISI and the madrassas deny these links (see several issues of *Wafaq al Madaris*) and therefore, it cannot be ascertained as to how many madrassas have increased due to the financial aid provided by foreign donors and the Pakistan army. The increase in the number of registered madrassas is as follows (for details of increase in provinces see Annexure 4).

Table 5.2
Sect-Wise Increase in the Number of Madrassas

Deobandi		Barelvi		Ahl-i-Hadith		Shia		Jamaat-i-Islami		Total	
1988	2002	1988	2002	1988	2002	1988	2002	1988	2002	1988	2002
1779	7000	717	1585	161	376	47	419	97*	500	2801	9880

Source: For 1988 see GoP 1988; for 2002 Report of Sindh Police in *Dawn* 16 Jan 2003. The other figures have been provided by the Central Boards of madrassas.* This figure in GoP 1988 was for 'Others' and not only for the Jamaat-i-Islami madrassas.

P.W. Singer gives the figure of 45,000 madrassas but quotes no source for this number (Singer 2001).

The Saudi Arabian organization, Harmain Islamic Foundation, is said to have helped the Ahl-i-Hadith and made them powerful. Indeed, the Lashkar-e-Tayyaba, an organization, which has been active in fighting in Kashmir, belongs to the Ahl-i-Hadith (Ahmed 2002: 10). In recent years, the Deobandi influence has increased as the Taliban were trained in their seminaries. However, contrary to popular belief, it is the other madrassas and not the Deobandi that have either registered in large numbers since 1988 or actually increased in number. The increase in percentages in the different madrassas of the major sub-sects or sects between 1988 and 2000 is as follows:

Table 5.3
Increase in the Madrassas between 1988 and 2000
Percentages

Deobandi	6
Barelvi	90
Ahl-i-Hadith	93
Shia	532
Others	Not known
Total	136

Source: Khalid 2002: 176.

However, we should remember that the number of Deobandi madrassas is the highest to begin with and these are the ones which are associated with militant policies and revivalist fervour.

THE SECTARIAN DIVIDE AMONG THE MADRASSAS

✓ Consequent to the disintegration of the Mughal empire and colonial rule, Muslims in India felt threatened, disillusioned and frustrated. Some, like Sayyid Ahmed of Rae Bareilly (1786-1831), responded militantly but were defeated. Others, like Sir Syed Ahmad Khan (1808-98) learnt English, entered the British bureaucracy and became junior partners of the British in the exercise of power. Still others, blaming Muslims themselves for their loss of power, tried to purify Islam in various ways. The Wahabis (also called Ahl-i-Hadith), the Deobandis, the Barelvis among the Sunnis as well as the Shias created madrassas to preserve and propagate what, in their view, was the correct interpretation of Islam. These madrassas are described below.

Deobandis

The madrassa at Deoband, a small town in the United Provinces (now Uttar Pradesh) of India, was established by Maulana Muhammad Qasim Nanautawi (1833-1877) and Maulana Rashid Ahmed Gangohi

(1829-1905). While earlier seminaries were loosely organized, Deoband had a rector (*sarparast*), a chancellor (*muhtamim*) and the chief instructor (*sadr mudarris*). Its income was derived from popular contributions and the curriculum was based on the Dars-i-Nizami developed by Mulla Nizam Uddin Sihalvi (d. 1748) at Farangi Mahal, a famous seminary of a family of Islamic scholars (ulema) in Lucknow (Robinson 2002). The Dars-i-Nizami emphasized studies based on human reasoning (*maqulat*) but at Deoband the traditional sciences, which were transmitted unchanged to the learner (*manqulat*) were emphasized. Thus Deoband taught much more hadith than the Dars-i-Nizami had originally prescribed.

The Deobandis opposed folk Islam in which intercession by saints occupied a major place. Seeking initiation in a mystic order was considered the path to salvation and miracles were seen as crucial and defining attributes of saints and prophets. They did not oppose mysticism altogether but did argue that adherence to the Islamic law (*Sharia*) was the path to mystical exaltation. They also opposed folk practices like that of fixing days for distributing food to gain spiritual merit and celebrating the anniversaries of religious personages (for details see Metcalf 1982).

The Darul Uloom at Deoband was established in 1867 and after a hundred years, it had produced 6,986 graduates and established 8,934 *maktabs* (schools) and madrassas (seminaries) teaching the Dars-i-Nizami. In 1967 the number of graduates from Pakistan was 3,191 (including those from East Pakistan) (Metcalf 1982: 110-1) while now the number of students exceeds 1, 02, 865 and the number of those who have appeared in the Alimia (M.A) examination is 4,676 . The number of registered madrassas in Pakistan is 7000, which shows how fast they have multiplied in recent years in this country (all these figures are from the central office of the Wafaq-ul-Madaris, Multan).

Barelvis

The Barelvi movement was inspired by Ahmed Raza Khan of Bareilly (1856-1921) who is highly revered by his followers (Sanyal 1996). The Barelvis justified the 'mediational, custom-laden Islam, closely tied to the intercession of the pirs of the shrines' (Metcalf 1982: 296). They believed that Prophet Muhammad (PBUH) was made of Divine Radiance (*Noor*) and had knowledge of the unknown (*Ilm ul Ghaib*).

The Deobandis and the Ahl-i-Hadith *ulema* challenged both these beliefs. Related to this was the debate on the issue of the *imkan-i-nazir*—the question whether God could make another person equal to Prophet Muhammad (PBUH). The Barelvis denied the possibility while the others did not. The Barelevi madrassas in Pakistan also teach the Dars-i-Nizami and appeal to the ordinary folk of the country (for the views of the Barelvis see Sanyal 1996).

Ahl-i-Hadith

The movement inspire   habi because, like Mohammad bin   audi Arabia, Sayyid Ahmed and h   and reform Islam. They claimed t   sprudence— Hanafi, Shafi, Hamb   nconformists (*ghair muqallid* = one who does not follow a fixed path) by their opponents. They used the term Jama'at Ahl-i-Hadith for themselves and appealed to the Government of India that the term Wahabi should not be used for them. The government 'ordered in 1886 that the term Wahabi should not be used in official correspondence' (Ahmed 1994: 203) but it is still used by many people in Pakistan.

[handwritten note: madrassahs were created against British rule & even now. They educate ppl against western ideas.]

The Ahl-i-Hadith madrassas also teach the Dars-i-Nizami but they emphasize the Quran and Hadith and oppose folk Islam and common practices like the anniversaries of saints, the distribution of food on religious occasions and popular mysticism.

Jamaat-i-Islami

The Jamaat-i-Islami is a revivalist political party created by Abul ala Maudoodi (also spelled Mawdudi) (1903-1979) whose life and achievements have been ably described by Syyed Vali Reza Nasr (1996).

Maudoodi believed in borrowing technology and other concepts from the West in order to empower the Islamic community. As such he favoured more modernist education than any of the orthodox organizers of the traditional madrassas. He did, however, also emphasize upon the refutation of Western culture and intellectual domination and, therefore, his anti-Western critique is more thorough, trenchant and appealing than that of the traditionalist seminarians (Maudoodi 1974).

In the Jamaat's madrassas the traditional texts are taught but politics, economics and history is also emphasized with a view to preparing the young ulema for confronting the ideas of the West.

Shia run Madrassas

Besides the Sunni run madrassas, there are also Shia run madrassas as mentioned earlier. The Shias believe that the successor of the Prophet (PBUH) was Ali Ibn-e-Abi Talib and not the first three caliphs whom Sunnis take to be his successors. They mourn the battle of Karbala, fought between the Prophet's grandson Hussain and the Umayyad caliph Yazid bin Muawiya in AD 680. This led to the strengthening of the supporters of Ali and the rise of Shia Islam which has been described very competently by S.H.M Jafri (1979).

All the madrassas, including those of the Shia, teach the Dars-i-Nizami though they do not use the same texts. They also teach their particular point of view (*madhab or maslak*) which clarifies and rationalizes the beliefs of the sect (Sunni or Shia) and sub-sect (Deobandi, Barelvi and Ahl-i-Hadith). Moreover, they train their students to refute what they consider heretical beliefs and some Western ideas. All madrassas teach modern subjects in some measure and with varying degrees of competence. Let us examine the teaching in the madrassas in some detail.

The Dars-i-Nizami

Before Mulla Nizam Uddin standardized the curriculum known as the Dars-i-Nizami, different teachers used different books to teach their students. Shah Abdul Rahim attempted to create a fixed curriculum. This was taught at the Madrassa-i-Rahimiya and it emphasized the *manqulat* (such as hadith). The Dars-i-Nazami on the other hand, emphasized the *maqulat*. Thus there were now more books on grammar, logic and philosophy than before (Sufi 1941: 68-75). According to Francis Robinson:

> The significance of the enhanced emphasis on ma'qulat in the Dars-i-Nizamiyya lies in part in the superior training it offered prospective lawyers, judges and administrators. The study of advanced books of logic,

> Philosophy and dialectics sharpened the rational faculties and, ideally, brought to the business of government men with better-trained minds and better-formed judgement (Robinson 2002: 53).

While this may have been the intention of Farangi Mahal's ulema, it is also true that the Arabic madrassas were far fewer (150) than the Persian schools (903) in 1850 (Edn. NWP: 1850), presumably because these offered a more thorough grounding in Persian which facilitated the entry of the pupils into administrative jobs. However, Farangi Mahal was established before the British created the category of 'Persian schools' and it does appear that the Dars-i-Nizami educated men were sought for employment outside the domain of religion at that time.

In Pakistan, however, the Dars-i-Nizami has been modified though the canonical texts are still there. In my view these texts are used as a symbol of continuity and identity. The madrassas saw themselves as preservers of Islamic identity and heritage during the colonial era when secular studies displaced the Islamic texts as well as the classical languages of the Indian Muslims—Arabic and Persian—from their privileged pedestal. Thus the madrassas, despite the desire to reform their courses, do not give up the canonical texts (for a debate on reform see IPS 1987). The greatest critic of the madrassa texts was Maulana Maududi who argued that, being based on memorization of medieval texts, the madrassas were not providing relevant education to the Muslim society (Maudoodi 1974).

However, though old books like *Sarf-e-Meer* and *Kafiya* remain in the course, easier and more modern books are used to supplement them. Arabic, for instance, is taught through modern and much easier books than the canonical works mentioned in the Dars-i-Nizami (for details see Rahman 2002: 106-108). The canonical texts are taught in Arabic but because students do not become competent in the language, they either memorize them or understand them from Urdu translations.

The Dars-i-Nizami has come to symbolize the stagnation and ossification of knowledge. It is taught through canonical texts through commentaries (*sharh*); glosses or marginal notes (*hashiya*) and super-commentaries (*taqarir*). There are commentaries upon commentaries explained by even more commentaries. For the South Asian students, who do not know Arabic well, they no longer explain the original text being themselves in Arabic. They have to be learned by heart, which makes students use only their memory not their analytical powers.

Indeed, the assumption on which the Dars functions is that the past was a golden age in which all that was best has already been written. What remains to the modern age is merely to preserve it.

It was this backward-looking nature of core madrassa texts that made Taha Hussain (1889-1973), the famous blind modernist scholar of Egypt, disillusioned with the Jamia Azhar in Cairo. According to Abdelrarshid Mahmoudi, the author of a book on Taha Hussain's education:

> On the collective level, entanglement in what was derivative and purely verbal, meant, among other things, the relegation of major and original works to oblivion. Thus a procedure whose sole raison d'etre was the conservation of tradition, resulted in a grave form of collective amnesia concerning what was best in Islamic culture, namely the classical heritage (Mahmoudi 1998: 20).

What was true of Jamia Azhar in 1902 (when Taha went to that seat of learning) is judged to be true of South Asian madrassas, or at least the Dars-i-Nizami component. Even now the judges are Arabic-knowing authorities such as Maudoodi and not just Western critics of the madrassas.

THE REFUTATION OF OTHER SECTS AND SUB-SECTS

Refutation (*Radd* in Urdu) has always been part of religious education. However, it is only in recent years that it has been blamed for the unprecedented increase in sectarian violence in Pakistan.

According to A.H. Nayyar 'The madrasahs have, not surprisingly, become a source of hate-filled propaganda against other sects and the sectarian divide has become sharper and more violent' (Nayyar 1998: 243). However, it appears that there was much more acrimonious theological debate among the Shias and Sunnis and among the Sunnis themselves during British rule than is common nowadays. The militancy in sectarian conflict cannot be attributed to the teaching in the madrassas though, of course, the awareness of divergent beliefs does create the potential for negative bias against people of other beliefs.

The theological debate (*munazra*) is taught to students in the madrassas. Barbara Metcalf describes the munazras between the Christians, Muslims and Arya Samajists (1982: 219-32) in her book. She says:

> The debates were, indeed, a form of social event, a public ritual, that took on new form and meaning in the late nineteenth century. In a society largely illiterate and equipped only minimally with modern forms of communication, they came to serve as a new forum for communicating issues at once religious and social (Metcalf 1982: 233).

They were also very bitter as the Deobandi-Barelvi *munazras* of 1928 collected in *Futoohat-e-Nomania* (Nomani 2002) illustrate. Moreover, the pioneers of the sects and sub-sects did indulge in refuting each other's beliefs. For instance Ahmed Raza Khan, the pioneer of the Barelvi school, wrote a series of *fatawa* (plural of *fatwa* = religious decree) against Sir Sayyid of Aligarh, the Shias, the Ahl-i-Hadith, the Deobandis and the Nadwat ul-'Ulama in 1896. These were published as *Fatawa al-Haramain bi-Rajf Nadwat al-Main* (1900) (Sanyal 1996: 203). The Barelvis, in turn, were refuted by their rivals. The followers of the main debaters sometimes exchanged invectives and even came to blows but never turned to terrorism as witnessed in Pakistan's recent history.

As the inculcation of sectarian bias is an offence, no madrassa teacher or administrator confessed to teaching any text refuting the beliefs of other sects. Maulana Mohammad Hussain, Nazim-e-Madrassa Jamiat us-Salfia (Ahl-i-Hadith) (Islamabad) said that comparative religions was taught in the final Almiya (MA) class and it did contain material refuting heretical beliefs. Moreover, Islam was confirmed as the only true religion, refuting other religions. The library did contain books refuting other sects and sub-sects but they were not prescribed in the syllabus. Maulana Mohammad Ishaq Zafar of the Jamia Rizvia Aiz ul Uloom (Barelvi) in Rawalpindi said that books against other sects were not taught. However, during the interpretation of texts the *maslak* was passed on to the student. Students of the final year, when questioned specifically about the teaching of the *maslak*, said that it was taught through questions and answers, interpretation of texts and sometimes some teachers recommended supplementary reading material specifically for the refutation of the doctrines of other sects and sub-sects.

In some cases, as in the Jamia Ashrafia, a famous Deobandi seminary of Lahore, an institution for publication, established in 1993, publishes 'only those articles and journals which are written by the scholars of Deoband school of thought.' (Hussain 1994: 42). Moreover, in writings, sermons, and conversation, the teachers refer to the pioneers of their own *maslak* so that the views of the sub-sect are internalized and become the primary way of thinking.

However, despite all denials, the printed syllabi of the following sects do have books to refute the beliefs of other sects. The Report on the Religious Seminaries (GOP 1988) lists several books of Deobandi madrassas to refute Shia beliefs including Maulana Mohammad Qasim's *Hadiyat ul Shia* which has been reprinted several times and is still in print. There are also several books on the debates between the Barelvis and the Deobandis and even a book refuting Maudoodi's views (GoP 1988: 73-74) The Barelvis have named only one book: *Rashidiya* under the heading of 'preparation for debates on controversial issues' (ibid., p.76). The Ahl-i-Hadith have given a choice of opting for any two of the following courses: the political system of Islam, the economic system of Islam, Ibn-e-Khaldun's *Muqaddamah*, the history of ideas and comparative religious systems. The Shia courses list no book on this subject.

Recently published courses list no book on *maslak* for the Deobandis. The Barelvis mention 'comparative religions' but no specific books. The Ahl-i-Hadith retain almost the same optional courses as before. The Shia madrassas list books that includes comparative religions; Of course, Shia beliefs are taught as the only true ones. Polemical pamphlets claiming that there are conspiracies against the Shias are available. Such pamphlets, warning about alleged Shia deviations from the correct interpretations of the faith, are also in circulation among Sunni madrassas and religious organizations.

Moreover, some guidebooks for teachers note that Quranic verses about controversial issues should be taught with great attention and students should memorize them. In one Barelvi book it is specified that teachers must make the students note down interpretations of the *ulema* of their sub-sect concerning beliefs and controversial issues so that students can use them later, i.e. as preachers and *ulema*.

The Jamaat-i-Islami syllabus (2002) mentions additional books by Maulana Maudoodi and other intellectuals of the Jamaat on a number of subjects including the Hadith. They also teach 'comparative religions'.

THE REFUTATION OF HERETICAL BELIEFS

One of the aims of the madrassas, ever since 1057 when Nizam ul Mulk established the famous madrassa at Baghdad, was to counter heresies within the Islamic world and outside influences, which could change or dilute Islam (Makdisi 1981: 7 and 17). Other religions are refuted in 'comparative religions' but there are specific books for heresies within the Islamic world. In Pakistan the *ulema* unite in refuting the beliefs of the Ahmedis (or Qaidianis) (for these views see Friedmann 1989). The Deoband course for the Aliya (BA) degree included five books refuting Ahmedi beliefs (GoP 1988: 71). The Barelvis prescribe no specific books. However, the *fatawa* of the pioneer, Ahmad Raza Khan, are referred to and they refute the ideas of the other sects and sub-sects. The Ahl-i-Hadith note that in 'comparative religions' they would refute the Ahmedi beliefs. The Shias too do not prescribe any specific books. The Jamaat-i-Islami's syllabus (2002) prescribes four books for the refutation of 'Qaidiani religion'. Besides the Ahmedis, other beliefs deemed to be heretical are also refuted. All these books are written in a polemical style and are in Urdu, which all madrassa students understand.

THE REFUTATION OF ALIEN PHILOSOPHIES

The earliest madrassas refuted Greek philosophy, which was seen as an intellectual invasion of the Muslim ideological space. Since the rise of the West, madrassas, and more so the revivalist movements outside the madrassas, refute Western philosophies. Thus there are books given in the reading lists for Aliya (BA) of 1988 by the Deobandis refuting capitalism, socialism, capitalism and feudalism. These books are no longer listed but they are in print and in the libraries of the madrassas. The Jamaat-i-Islami probably goes to great lengths—judging from its 2002 syllabus—to make the students aware of Western domination, the exploitative potential of Western political and economic ideas, and the disruptive influence of Western liberty and individualism on Muslim societies. Besides Maudoodi's own books on all subjects relating to the modern world, a book on the conflict between Islam and Western ideas (Nadvi nd) is widely available.

These texts, which may be called *Radd*-texts, may not be formally taught in most of the madrassas as the *ulema* claim, but they are being printed which means they are in circulation. They may be given as supplementary reading material or used in arguments by teachers, which are probably internalized by the students. In any case, being in Urdu rather than Arabic, such texts can be comprehended rather than merely memorized. As such, without formally being given the centrality which the Dars-i-Nizami has, the opinions these texts disseminate—opinions against other sects, sub-sects, views seen as heretical by the ulema, Western ideas—may be the major formative influence on the minds of madrassa students. Thus, while it is true that education in the madrassa produces religious, sectarian, sub-sectarian and anti-Western bias, it may not be true to assume that this bias automatically translates into militancy and violence of the type Pakistan has experienced. For that to happen other factors: the arming of religious young men to fight in Afghanistan and Kashmir; the state's clampdown on free expression of political dissent during Ziaul Haq's martial law; the appalling poverty of rural, peripheral areas and urban slums etc.—must be taken into account.

As for teaching modern subjects, the Ahl-i-Hadith madrassas have been teaching Pakistan studies, English, Mathematics and General Science for a long time (GoP 1988: 85). The Jamaat-i-Islami also teaches secular subjects. The larger Deobandi, Barelvi and Shia madrassas too have made arrangements for teaching secular subjects including basic computer skills. However, teachers approved of by the *ulema* or some of the *ulema* themselves do the teaching. Thus the potential for secularization of these subjects, which is small in any case, is reduced to nothingness.

MADRASSAS, POVERTY AND SOCIOECONOMIC CLASS

Land grants and wealthy patrons in medieval India supported madrassas. They have always supported the poor and the lifestyle of the *ulema* were spartan and closer to the poorer strata of society than the affluent ones. Maulana Abdul Ali Bahr al-Ulam of Farangi Mahal, for instance, 'used in their support all but Rs 40 of the Rs 1000 monthly stipend granted by Nawab Walajah. His 'wife and family suffered and complained, as did those of his grandson, Jamal al-Din, who suffered in a similar way' (Robinson 2002: 81). Barbara Metcalf in her study of Deoband tells us that the pioneers of that seminary took no, or very modest salaries, and 'lived like poor men' (1982:

167). The average expense of Deoband on each graduate between 1867 to 1967 was Rs 1,314, which is modest by any criterion (Metcalf 1982: 111). The Ahl-i-Hadith madrassas, which were patronized by wealthy people in British India, nevertheless lived in the same frugal manner (Ahmed 1994).

Madrassas in Pakistan are also financed by voluntary charity provided by the bazaar businessmen, Muslims settled in Western countries and others who believe that they are earning great merit by contributing to them. Some of them are also given financial assistance by foreign governments—the Saudi government is said to help the Ahl-i-Hadith seminaries and the Iranian government the Shia ones— but there is no proof of this assistance. And even if it does exist, it goes only to a few madrassas whereas the vast majority of them are run on charity (*zakat* = alms, *khairat* = charity, *atiat* = gifts etc).

The government of Pakistan gives financial assistance to the madrassas for modernizing textbooks, including secular subjects in the curricula and introducing computers. In 2001-2 a total of Rs 1,654,000 was given to all madrassas which accepted this help. As the number of students is 1,065,277 this amounts to Rs 1.55 per student per year. An additional aid of Rs 30.45 million is promised for providing computers and changing the syllabi in 2003-4 and this will come to Rs 28.60 per student per year (these figures are from IPS 2002 table 1.17 and 1.19). However, since all madrassas do not accept financial help from the government, the money is not distributed evenly as the above calculations might suggest.

According to the Jamia Salfia of Faisalabad, the annual expenditure on the seminary, which has about 700 students, is 40,00,000 rupees. Another madrassa, this time a Barelvi one, gave roughly the same figure for the same number of students. This comes to Rs 5,714 per year (or Rs 476 per month), which is an incredibly small amount of money for education, books, board and lodging. As the madrassas generally do not charge tuition fees—though they do charge small admission fees, not exceeding Rs 400—they attract very poor students who would not receive any education otherwise. According to Fayyaz Hussain, a student who completed his ethnographic research on Jamia Ashrafia of Lahore in 1994, students joined the madrassa for the following reasons:

Table 5.3
Reasons Given by the Students for Joining Madrassas
Percentages

Economic	48.95
Social	40.63
Religious	5.71
Educational	3.12
Political	2.09

Source: Hussain 1994: 84.

The author has not explained the categories nor is it known exactly what questions were asked of the students. According to Singer, the 'Dar-ul-Uloom Haqqania, one of the most popular and influential madrassahs (it includes most of the Afghani Taliban leadership among its alumni) has a student body of 1500 boarding students and 1000 day students, from six-years old upwards. Each year over 15,000 applicants from poor families vie for its 400 open spaces (Singer 2001). According to a survey conducted by Mumtaz Ahmad in 1976 'more than 80 per cent of the madrassa students in Peshawar, Multan, and Gujranwala were found to be sons of small or landless peasants, rural artisans, or imams of the village mosques. The remaining 20 per cent came from families of small shopkeepers and rural laborers' (quoted from Ahmad 2000: 185). I have also observed that many students, upon probing, confessed that their parents had admitted them in the madrassas because they could not afford to feed them and educate them in the government schools. Even such students, while making this confession, also insist that they are in the madrassas because of their love for Islam.

In the survey of December 2002 and January 2003, madrassa students and teachers were asked about their income. Many did not reply these questions but those who did suggest that they mostly (76.62 per cent) belong to poor sections of society (see Annexure 1 for details). The teachers of the madrassas also mostly (61.11 per cent) belong to the same socio-economic class as their students (see Annexure 1 for details). The madrassas provide sustenance for all these poor people.

In short, the madrassas perform the role of the welfare state in the country. As a result, their influence on rural people and the poorer sections of the urban proletariat will continue to increase as poverty increases.

POVERTY AND THE ROOTS OF RELIGIOUS VIOLENCE

While the connection between poverty and religious violence can only be speculated, the proposition does have empirical backing. Qasim Zaman tells us, for instance, that in Jhang—the birthplace of the militant Sunni organization called the Sipah-i-Sahaba—the proportion of Shias in the affluent urban middle class is higher than other areas of Pakistan. Moreover, the feudal gentry too has many Shia families. Thus, the Sipah-i-Sahaba appeals to the interests of the ordinary people who are oppressed by the rich and the influential. Indeed, Maulana Haqq Nawaz, the fiery preacher who raised much animosity against the Shias, was 'himself a man of humble origin' and 'had a reputation for being much concerned with the welfare of the poor and the helpless, and he was known to regularly spend time at government courts helping out poor illiterate litigants' (Zaman 2002: 125).

Another leader of the Sipah-i-Sahaba, Maulana Isar al-Qasimi (1964-1991), also preached in Jhang. He too denounced the Shia magnates of the area, and the peasants, terrorized by the feudal magnates, responded to him as if he were a messiah. Even shopkeepers rejoiced in the aggressive Sunni identity he helped create. When the Shia feudal lords attacked and burnt some defiant Sunni shops, this identity was further radicalized (Zaman 2002: 127).

In the same manner, the Muslim radicals in the Philippines attack the social and economic privilege of the dominant Christian majority. Indeed, Islamist movements from Turkey to Indonesia talk of the poor and the oppressed and sometimes do take up their cause. This has won them votes in Turkey where they have been suppressed by the secular military. It was also a major factor for mobilization in Iran against the Shah who was seen as rich, wasteful, corrupt and decadent. So, though difficult to demonstrate, Islamic militancy—whether by radicalized madrassa students or members of Islamist or Jihadi groups in Pakistan—has an element of class conflict. It is, at least in some part, a reaction of the have-nots against the haves. This is a dangerous trend for the country because madrassa students are taught to be intolerant of religious minorities and are hawkish about Kashmir. Since they are also from poor socioeconomic backgrounds, they express their sense of being cheated by society in the idiom of religion. This gives them the self-righteousness to fight against the oppressive and unjust system in the name of Islam.

THE WORLDVIEW OF MADRASSA STUDENTS

The madrassa students are the most intolerant of all other student groups in Pakistan. They are also the most supportive of an aggressive foreign policy. In the survey of 2002-3, they responded to questions about these issues as follows:

Table 5.4
Militancy Among Madrassa Students in 2003 (N=142)
(%)

What should be Pakistan's Priorities?	Yes	No	Don't Know
1. Take Kashmir away from India by an open war?	59.86	31.69	8.45
2. Take Kashmir away from India by supporting Jihadi groups to fight with the Indian army?	52.82	32.39	14.79
3. Support Kashmir cause through peaceful means only (i.e. no open war or sending Jihadi groups across the Line of Control)	33.80	54.93	11.27

Source: Annexure 2.

The views of the teachers were even more militant:

Table 5.5
Militancy Among Madrassa Teachers (N=27) (%)

		Yes	No	Don't Know
1.	Open War	70.37	22.22	7.41
2.	Jihadi Groups	59.26	29.63	11.11
3.	Peaceful means	29.63	66.67	3.70

Source: Annexure 2.

What needs explanation is that the madrassas, which were basically conservative institutions before the Afghan-Soviet War of the 1980s, are now ideologically activist and sometimes militant. According to Peter L. Bergen, author of a book on Osama bin Laden and his al-Qaeda group: 'nowhere is bin Laden more popular than in Pakistan's madrassas, religious schools from which the Taliban draw many of its recruits' (Bergen 2001: 150). Even with the end of Taliban rule in Afghanistan, the madrassas have plenty of zealous young people who can potentially act as crusaders against both Western interests and the moderate regimes, both military and civilian, whom they perceive as the allies of the West (for Central Asian parallels see Ahmed Rashid's [2002] excellent book on militant Islamic movements in that part of the world).

General Pervez Musharraf's military government, in an attempt to control religious extremism, made two laws to control the madrassas. The first was aimed at bringing the madrassas into the mainstream by introducing secular subjects in them. The Pakistan Madrassah Education (Establishment and Affiliation of Model Dini Madaris) Board Ordinance 2001 was promulgated on 18 August 2001. According to the Education Sector Reforms (GoP 2002c) three model institutions were established: one at Karachi, Sukkur and Islamabad. Their curriculum 'includes subjects of English, Mathematics, Computer Science, Economics, Political Science, Law and Pakistan Studies for its different levels (GoP 2002c: 23). These institutions were not welcomed by the *ulema* (for opposition from the *ulema* see *Wafaq ul Madaris* No. 6: Vol. 2, 2001). After this another law was introduced to control the entry of foreigners in the madrassas and keep a check on them. This law—Voluntary Registration and Regulation Ordinance 2002—has, however, been rejected by most of the madrassas that want no state interference in their affairs (see *Wafaq ul Madaris* Vol. 3 No. 9, 2002 and unstructured interviews of the *ulema*). Indeed, according to Singer, '4,350, about one-tenth, agreed to be registered and the rest simply ignored the statute' (Singer 2001). The number of those who did not register is not known.

The madrassas became militant when they were used by the Pakistani state to fight in Afghanistan during the Soviet occupation and then in Kashmir in order to force India to leave the state. Pakistan's claim on Kashmir, as discussed by many including Alastair Lamb (1977), has led to conflict with India and the Islamic militants or Jihadis, who have entered the fray since 1989. The United States indirectly, and sometimes directly, helped in creating militancy among the clergy. For instance, special textbooks in Darri (Afghan Persian) and Pashto were written at the University of Nebraska-Omaha with a USAID grant in the 1980s (Stephens and Ottaway 2002: Sec A, p. 1). American arms and money flowed to Afghanistan through Pakistan's Inter Services Intelligence as several books indicate (see Cooley 1999). At that time, all this was done to defeat the Soviet Union. Later, while Pakistan's military continued to use the militant Islamists in Kashmir, the United States was much alarmed by them—not without reason as the events of 9/11 demonstrated later. After this catastrophic incident in which more than three thousand people died in New York, the Americans tried to understand the madrassas better. P.W. Singer, an analyst in the Brookings Institute who has been referred to earlier, wrote that there were 10-15 per cent 'radical' madrassas which teach anti-American rhetoric, terrorism and even impart military training (Singer 2001). No proof for these claims was offered but they are credible given the fact that madrassa teachers often say that the USA is at war with Islam.

Apart from the madrassas proper, religious parties—such as Lashkar-e-Tayyaba, Jaish-e-Mohammed and Harkat-ul-Mujahidin— print militant literature that is circulated among the madrassas and other institutions. According to chapter-3 of a book entitled *Ideas on Democracy, Freedom and Peace in Textbooks* (2003), Ad-Dawah uses textbooks for English in which many questions and answers refer to war, weapons, blood and victory:

> The students studying in jihadi schools are totally brain washed right from the very beginning. The textbooks have been authored to provide only one-dimensional worldview and restrict the independent thought process of children (Liberal Forum 2003: 72).

Although these parties have been banned, their member are said to have dispersed all over Pakistan, especially in the madrassas. The madrassas, then, may be the potential centres of Islamic militancy in Pakistan.

STORY

The Making of a Mulla

Nabi Baksh [not his real name] was born in southern Punjab near Bahawalpur. As camels trudged past in majestic aloofness, the scorching heat and suffocating dust stirred up Nabi's earliest memories. But he could hardly be either majestic or aloof as he had to compete for pieces of loaves and *dal* (lentil soup) with his brothers and sisters. Then his father died and his mother had to survive by working in the house of the local feudal lord. And if there was a memory of that infancy it was of the hollering feudal master; the stolen morsels from the kitchen in his mother's *dupatta* (scarve) and hunger and always the stifling heat.

Then someone put him in the madrassa. He missed his mother, but the gnawing, ever-present hunger was gone. The Mullaji gave him food morning, afternoon and evening. And, incredibly enough, every day— every blessed day—the food appeared as if it descended like manna out of the heavens.

But life was not all heavens for one had to study. No more running wild listening to the pealing bells of the camels. Instead there were lessons and if one did not know the lesson, the mullah caught one by the ear. But mostly one was let off lightly—only Mullah Gul Khan, a pathan from the Khyber, was a tyrant. If he caught you he made you squeal; and he taught the Arabic language.

But Nabi Baksh did well and graduated from the *maktab* (school) to the madrassa. Here the studies were all but mind-boggling. He was lost in Arabic grammar, the rules of which were in forbidding Arabic verse. The margins and the commentaries were so many and so difficult that he would have given up but for the memory of the pangs of hunger and the red-eyed feudal grandee who was waiting to pounce on him outside the madrassa. He did pounce upon his mother, he knew, but what could he do about it.

Besides, he knew he would get some kind of employment when he graduated from the madrassa. Above all, now that he was growing up, he was beginning to feel proud of his position. He would become a *maulvi*, maybe an *alim*, and that would be an honour. After all, instead of being a servant of the feudal lord, he would be a servant of Allah. He started finding this newfound source of pride most satisfactory.

Then came preachers who never smiled. They came from some far off, hush hush place, where they had been fighting the infidels. But they found fault with his name, which meant 'one who had been gifted by the Prophet of Islam [Peace be Upon Him]'. They agreed that life and birth were the gifts of God and gave him a new name: Allah Baksh. This was no problem except that his mother found it unsettling. But then wasn't she only an ignorant peasant woman? Or so he felt.

But the strangers wanted him to go with them to fight in a jihad—a holy war against the infidels. He almost went but one of his teachers pointed out what an excellent student he was. Someone, after all, had to serve Islam by interpreting and disseminating the word of God. The dour strangers mumbled but remained content with those whom they had recruited. Among them were some of his best friends—boys he had learnt grammar with rocking his body to and fro in a method that they called *takrar*. Allah Baksh saw only one of them again and he never smiled nor did he talk to anyone again.

Allah Baksh become a teacher in the madrassa and was filled with incredulous wonder when they gave him a salary of two thousand rupees in cash. This was newfound power that gave him freedom; he had heard about this from the grim-faced recruiters for the jihad but had never thaught he would find. But it was short lived because his mother married him off and now for the first time in his life, he learned that food cost money and there were such things as electricity bills. And then, unprepared though both the parents were, there were children who consumed incredible amounts of money. But as the boys grew up he sent them to the madrassa; as for the girls, he waited for them to turn fourteen so that they could be given away to their husbands—again, perhaps, from the madrassa.

6

HIGHER EDUCATION

COLLEGES

Colleges are institutions of higher education that serve as higher secondary schools (classes 11 and 12); traditional undergraduate universities in the West (offering, however, a BA of two years instead of the usual three); and the traditional Pakistani university (offering MA degrees). These are controlled by the provincial or the federal governments unlike the universities that are autonomous. According to the *Economic Survey of Pakistan* (GoP 2003) there are 925 colleges with an enrollment of 770,000 students out of which the number of female students are 378,000. These figures are for the year 2001-2 and the number of private colleges is not given. However, according to the UGC, there were thirty-five colleges in the private sector in 1998 (UGC 1999). There is a controversy going on, at the time of writing (June 2003), as to whether the government should or should not privatize the colleges. In late March, when the Forman Christian College of Lahore was handed back to the Presbyterian Church, which had originally established it, the new principal, Dr Peter Armacost, was attacked by 300 angry students who were protesting this decision. The students' point of view was that fees would be raised and the college would become unaffordable for them (Khan 2003: 4). Eventually, the authorities prevailed. The government seems to feel that it cannot provide quality education to so many students so some of its liabilities should be passed on to the private sector.

The public colleges are segregated according to gender. In the federal capital, and other federal territories as well, they are controlled by the army. All other colleges are controlled by directorates of education and are, therefore, firmly under the control of the civil and the military bureaucracy. The faculty is recruited by the public service commission and usually possess a simple master's degree. Members

of the faculty are then promoted mostly on the basis of seniority—
though recently those who hold higher degrees have been encouraged
to move up the promotion ladder till they become principals. Up to the
1970s college lecturers were class-2 officers of the provincial
government while army and central superior services officers were
class-1 in status. Thus, the prestige and status of college lecturers was
lower than that of the officers of the state and also lower than that of
university faculty who were not within the government's 'caste system'
of classes 1, 2, 3 and 4.

Since teaching college is not prestigious it attracts even less talented
people—or at least those who do not initially do well in other
examinations, such as civil services examinations, even if they were
talented—than the universities do. College students, coming from all
social classes, take college life to be a time of relaxation, fun and little
study. There are always some good teachers but there are many more
who are indifferent. The students, mostly from Urdu-medium schools,
learn from each other and from some of the few inspiring teachers.
Here they discover that lectures are in English while they have always
been taught in Urdu. After a few months, however, they learn to make
sense of this and some do very well in the prestigious competitive
examinations for high state jobs, find jobs abroad and even become
scholars and scientists of renown.

The intermediate colleges are really extensions of the schools, but
the two years a student stays here are the years of transition from the
Urdu-medium to the partly English-medium type of study. After this
students either go to the professional colleges—engineering and
medical—or into the degree colleges. The BA/B.Sc. courses, too, are
of two year duration and, of course, sub-standard by both British and
American standards. These two years, however, are seen as preparation
for the Master's degree which is supposed to be more challenging.
This is when play is supposed to end and serious study begins. The
courses leading to a Master's degree, however, are generally taken in
the university though colleges have started giving these degrees and
all big colleges in the cities have quite a number of MA classes now.

This is the state of affairs at present. Despite proposals to increase
the duration of study for a BA, it still remains at two years. College is
still a time of new found freedom (at least for boys) and relaxation.
And even now college teaching is not very prestigious nor is one
required to do any research or take any examination for getting
promoted. However, changes are coming. Firstly, private colleges and

universities are taking away the products of elitist schools so that the educational apartheid does not end in college but carries on forever. Secondly, most good students, especially boys, are attracted to information technology, business studies and other job-oriented subjects. This trend was always there but the number of such pragmatic, capital-generating subjects has increased and so has the competition for jobs. This makes colleges less attractive for the rich, the bright and the more enterprising (or more ambitious) of our youth.

At the moment, colleges have large areas but their buildings are dilapidated. The furniture is old and broken. The library is a depressing place with locked cupboards and not many new books. Academic journals are not known to most of the faculty members nor have students heard of them even when they study at the bachelors and masters levels. Apart from the sub-standard faculty with no research orientation, the state spends very little money on colleges. This is suggested by the following facts about the colleges of the Rawalpindi district in 2003.

Table 6.1
Cost Per Student Per Year and Other Facts about Colleges
(Rawalpindi District, 2003)

	Male	Female	Total
Colleges	9	20	29
Enrollment	11,048	20,402	31,450
Faculty members	389	610	999
Faculty/student ratio	28 students per faculty	34 per faculty	32 per faculty
Budget			Rs 251 million
Cost per student per year	-	-	Rs 9,572
Cost to the state (per student per year)	-	-	Rs 7,981

Source: Office of the District Executive officer (Education), Rawalpindi.

The cost per student per year in the federal governments colleges is Rs 18,756 and they are somewhat better than the colleges under the provincial government where most ordinary students study. There are thirty-three colleges in the cantonments with about 15,000 students, and they too are better than the ordinary colleges.

It is difficult to suggest what should be done to improve the colleges. Perhaps, with the low salaries public-funded college offer, it would be difficult to attract the kind of faculty who will make a real improvement. However, if incentives are offered and the faculty is given examinations in their specialization for each promotion, some improvement is possible. Colleges need not be affiliated with universities. Instead, the government should create a central body (perhaps called the Council of College Education) that should ensure uniformity of academic standards; make curricula and hire faculty members. All examinations at the bachelors' level should be held by this central body. This will reduce the burden on the universities which, at present, give degrees to institutions bearing their name but having a very different faculty than their own. The bachelors' degree can be of three years, but then most jobs should encourage graduates, rather than people with higher qualifications, to join them. This policy will also decrease the burden on the universities to which we turn now.

UNIVERSITIES

While we are in the twenty-first century, most of the public universities of the country are stuck in the middle of the nineteenth century almost when they were established first in 1857 (the University of Calcutta) by the British rulers of India. Meanwhile, a number of private universities, run by private entrepreneurs as well as institutions associated with the armed forces, are proliferating in all cities of Pakistan. The rest of this chapter is meant to give a brief history of the public universities in Pakistan: to find out what their condition is at present; and, most importantly, to suggest ways to improve the public universities. This last objective is not part of the purely scholarly objective of providing value-free knowledge. Therefore, these proposals for reform of the universities are given in the chapter on recommendations which, of course, may be criticized and changed by others. I must confess that I am serious about the following ideals regarding academia: academic freedom; self-governance by academics; diversity in subjects taught, especially in social sciences and humanities; and a commitment to an intellectual space where all ideas can be freely discussed. It is with these values in mind that this chapter should be read.

SECTION 1

In the Dispatch of 1857, the Directors of the East India Company, who effectively ruled India by this time, conveyed the order that universities be established in India (Richey 1922: 371). They were not to be academically prestigious. Hence it was specified that the examination for common degrees was not to be 'as difficult as that for the senior government scholarships' and 'the standard required should be such as to command respect without discouraging the efforts of deserving students' (ibid., 372). Among the reasons for establishing universities was that many British officers felt that the cost of running the administration would decrease if the lower jobs were given to Indians. Moreover, as James Sullivan testified before a Parliamentary Committee in 1832, the Indians were alienated from British rule by the fact that they were excluded 'from all offices of trust and emolument and from the position in the administration of the country, civil and military, which they occupied under own princes' (Sullivan 1832). A large number of respondents agreed that, for various reasons, Indians should be educated—educated to be Westernized—and employed under British superiors. In a letter of 29 September 1830 to the Bengal Presidency, the directors of the company expressed their 'earnest wish and hope' to 'see them qualified for situations of higher importance and trust' and, for this purpose, to 'rely chiefly on their becoming, through a familiarity with European Literature and science, imbued with the ideas and feeling of civilized Europe' (in Basu 1952: 303). Thus, even before Macaulay had put it in his well known Minute in 1835, British policy was to westernize the Indian elite.

But in England the most prestigious universities, Oxford and Cambridge, were autonomous institutions. They had been established by the coming together of masters and students. For instance C.E. Mallet, a historian of the University of Oxford, writes: 'The Universitas, the whole body of Masters or students there collected, began to have something like a corporate existence, to adopt customs, to claim privileges, to form an organization of its own' (Mallet 1924:

Vol. 1: 2-3). Here is a little more detailed, account of the development of the medieval European universities.

It is impossible to give the exact dates of the origin of all medieval universities, because many of them arose from more or less informal congregations of scholars. At Salerno famous physicians were already teaching during the ninth century, before the university became internationally famous as a medical center in the eleventh century. At the same time systematic legal studies were being pursued at Bologna, which became the leading school of law. During the twelfth century the University of Paris developed from schools connected with the cathedral on the Ile de la Cite. Oxford and Cambridge can also be traced back to the twelfth century. In the thirteenth and fourteenth centuries the universities of Valladoid, Seville, and Salamanca developed in Spain. Prague was officially chartered in 1347, Cracow in 1364, Heidelberg in 1385, Cologne in 1388, Erfurt in 1379, Leipzig, a secession from Prague, in 1409, Louvain in 1426, and Budapest in 1475. (Ulich 1965: 46).

These universities were ruled by the faculty (except in Bologna where students had more power); they were autonomous, neither subservient to the state nor to the barons nor even to the Church and, consequently, they had more academic freedom than we would expect any institution to possess in that age of powerful feudal lords and a very powerful Church. Indeed, for about a century or so the university was a place of adventure. Unorthodox topics, ideas, theories were investigated and discussed. 'The whole world of knowledge as it was then known was to be explored—no facet of it was to be forbidden' (Ross 1976: 7). These ideals would change with time as Church and state moved to curb the university and its ideal of self-governance and academic freedom. However, these still remain a part of the core beliefs of traditional academics. Indeed, in the Islamic world, too, self-governance and independence from the state is very much part of the ideals of the madrassa system of education. The *ulema* in Iran, India and Pakistan actively assert their independence and are still committed to self-governance.

In the Islamic world, the grand madrassa (*Jamia* University) began as a theological seminary in the tenth century. A famous madrassa was established by Nizam ul Mulk in 1067 in Baghdad (Makdisi 1981:31). Even earlier, the Fatimid Caliphs had established Al-Azhar in Cairo. This later developed into the most prestigious Islamic seat of learning in the world. Though ruled by the faculty, the madrassas began as and remained Islamic seminaries. They never claimed to foster freedom of thought. Moreover, while the madrassas might have inspired the institution of the charitable college in Europe, it was distinct from that corporate body that came to be known as the university. Thus George Makdisi points out that 'Muslim education was simply not organized into a university system, but rather into a college system' (Makdisi 1981:293).

Gradually, the universities became seminaries of the Church as well as finishing schools for the gentry. They also came to be financially supported, and in some ways influenced, by the state. However, even by the nineteenth century, the universities in England, notably Oxford and Cambridge, were highly elitist and not subordinate to the bureaucracy of the state. Indeed, Sheldon Rothblatt tells us that Cambridge dons did not appeal to the state for funds even if they wanted them for fear of losing their independence. It was not, however, true that they always used their independence for the good of society in general or even of the elite. For instance, in the nineteenth century, and even up till to day, Oxbridge gave pride of place to the classics. At Cambridge, the question whether Greek was to be optional or compulsory was put to the vote in 1905 and 'optional Greek was defeated by a margin of approximately five hundred votes' (Rothblatt 1968: 254). But, whether they used it for good or not, this tradition of independence made academics confident, fearless and not subservient to the state. Such a psychological attitude had its negative side, of course. It could lead to academic snobbery and disdain for social pressure. But its positive side was that academics did not feel powerless, inferior or subordinate to the state's functionaries. They could reform themselves—as they did eventually—and in their research publications they did not feel it necessary to tow the official line. So the concept of academic freedom grew and flourished.

In the United States, however, boards of non-academics—clergymen in the beginning and businessmen later—controlled the universities. Academics resented their control and tried to wrest powers from them. According to Thorstein Veblen:

The final discretion in the affairs of the seats of learning is entrusted to men who have proved their capacity for work that has nothing in common with the higher learning.....their pecuniary surveillance comes in the main to an interference with the academic work, the merits of which these men of affairs on the governing board are in no special degree qualified to judge' (Veblen 1965: 65-69).

But between 1820 and 1920 power did shift to the faculty or, at least, to the famous scholars among them because America then wanted to build famous universities, and the decision-makers reluctantly came to realize that this could not happen without giving both money and power to these famous people. By the 1950s faculty had much power, but the battle for academic freedom is ongoing as manifest even today: those who disagree with the Iraq War have met with disapproval despite claims of academic freedom (for the comparison of the development of the concept of academic freedom in Britain, Canada and the United States see Ross 1976: chapter 8).

In India, a conquered country academic freedom was feared. Hence the universities were not to be governed by academics nor were they completely free of the administrative control, or at least the influence, of the higher bureaucracy. Thus, the act establishing the University of Calcutta declared that the governor-general would be the chancellor and the chief justice of the supreme court, the vice chancellor of the University. Its fellows would include the Lieutenant Governor of Bengal and the North-Western Provinces, the Bishop of Calcutta, and Members of the Supreme Council of India (Act No. 11 of 1975 in Richey 1922: 410-11)

As if this were not enough to keep the universities entirely under the government's thumb, they also lacked both students and faculty in the beginning. They were merely affiliating bodies on the model of the University of London. This meant that they only took examinations while the actual teaching took place in affiliated colleges. The college faculty was part of the civil service with all the disadvantages of that status but few of the advantages. As Irene Gilbert and Edward Shils have pointed out, Indian academics have few traditions of autonomy, creating a mentality of subordination (Gilbert 1972; Shils 1970). The advantages: power, high salary, prestige, and privileges, that the Indian Civil Service (ICS) and army officers enjoyed, were missing. Permanence of tenure turned out to be a disadvantage, as academics had no incentive to do research.

Whether intended or not, the effect of creating state controlled affiliating universities was that academics never got the confidence to challenge the government. Being subordinate members of the elitist bureaucracy, they mentally accepted its authority and its moral claim to legitimate exercise of power even in academic matters. In any case, as Shils shows, governors often kept warning academics to eschew politics (Shils 1970: 194-6). In short, the colonial state produced a colonial university—one which did not have the psychological, economic, social, or legal potential to confront the powers that be. Recruitment to the universities—even when they became teaching universities—was faulty. Almost all jobs and power were controlled, or at least influenced, by the British bureaucracy. Indians, already in awe of the arbitrary powers of Mughal feudal grandees, now came to be overawed by the British district officers.

The aristocratic Indians pined for an officer's uniform and the educated ones for the letters ICS after their names. Thus there was a brain drain from higher education to administration. This, as Edward Shils tells us, is still true about India:

> I have not encountered one Indian academic who entered on his career under the pressure or the preferences of his elders. Parents encourage their offspring to enter government services, medicine, engineering and law but not university and college teaching (Shils 1970: 177).

Insofar as entry to Pakistani universities is concerned, this is probably true even now. At least as far as colleges are concerned it seems certainly true. However, some intellectuals and radical minded young people, who do not like the bondage of government service, do join the universities in Pakistan. But such people are a mere handful and even they sometimes tend to drift away to Western or private universities or NGOs.

The other deleterious effects of over developing the state and conferring such inordinate prestige on the ICS were that the bureaucracy became a self-regarding and self-sustaining pressure group. Thus it remains, even today in Pakistan, a powerful opponent of any reformist proposal to make academia so autonomous, powerful or financially better off that its own higher status is undermined. Worst of all, however, was the psychologically crippling effect this lack of 'recognition'—to use a word made current by Fukuyama—had on brilliant academics. The brilliant person's 'sense of self-worth and the demand that it be recognized' (Fukuyama 1992: 181) can lead to frustration, anger, mortification, or dejection. No wonder, brilliant people either abandoned the academic life; closed their minds to outside reality by becoming monastic recluses or wasted their lives in idleness consoling themselves by the fact that if the society gave them so little they got some of their own back by doing very little work.

All of these were defense mechanisms but the one of closing the mind is so pervasive that it needs more comment. The academic feels, or professes to feel, that he is a moral mentor—something of the *sufi pir* (mystic mentor) or a *guru*. In a 'sacred' profession; he professes to despise wealth and power. Thus many Pakistani academics, and other Pakistanis as well, say that academics should not seek the kind of privileges or consumer goods that other members of the elite can legitimately seek. As Shils puts it for India but with equal relevance for Pakistan:

> It [public opinion] respects saintliness—intermittently—and it defers to power, but it does not respect hard and persistent intellectual work and it shows little concern for the conditions under which an academic can be effective. The tasks of academics entail neither the exercise of power nor the practice of saintliness. An atmosphere of opinion which admires these is not likely to contribute to the well-being and fruitfulness of a profession which involves neither of these. This state of opinion which derogates the academic profession helps to confirm itself, and it produces no positive results (Shils 1970: 173-4).

Such an attitude—the 'saint syndrome' as I call it—does not lead to academics becoming any different from other people, but it does make them more hypocritical and more frustrated than others. Moreover, the academic profession is unable to attract able young people.

Another characteristic of the colonial university was that it was supposed to teach and not to conduct research. The faculty was seen, and saw itself, as teachers. Indeed, the term 'academic' was never used, nor is it in use today in South Asia. The major reason for this seems to be that in the nineteenth century English universities were teaching, rather than research, oriented institutions. Only German universities emphasized research. James Morgan Hart, a visitor from America to Germany, commented thus on the German professor:

> The professor is not a teacher, in the English sense of the term; he is a specialist. He is not responsible for the success of his hearers. He is responsible only for the quality of his instruction. His duty begins and ends with himself (Hart 1874: 22).

But the Oxbridge professor was a teacher and not necessarily a scholar in 1874 when this was written. In India, the professorial title was further devalued, more than it ever was in England, because college lecturers appropriated it. This degradation of the professorate has political implications as well.

Teachers, however influential among their students, have no influence upon the educated public. They merely disseminate the knowledge produced by others without carrying out creative, original research themselves. Scholars, on the other hand, produce knowledge. They are recognized to be highly erudite and intelligent members of society in general. They can, especially if they choose to, have much influence and are looked upon with admiration if their work is sufficiently impressive. Teachers, therefore, could not have the intellectual prestige to stand up to the Raj bureaucracy whereas scholars could. Thus, whether it was planned or not, the result of filling colleges and universities with teachers rather than prestigious scholars was that the Raj had little to fear from the Indian academia.

Higher education, then, was a depressed sector of the society—a sector that had never been allowed to take off. Did it take off then when British rule ended in 1947 and Pakistan, a country carved out of British India with a Muslim majority, emerged on the map of the world? Let us turn to the next section for the answer.

SECTION 2

Pakistani Universities in the Post-Colonial Era

The universities retained their colonial character after 1947. As in colonial times, it was the official sector—the military and the bureaucracy in that order—that got more financial support, more power and more prestige than academia. Whether this was because the independent scholar with public prestige and command of facts was seen as a threat by the ruling elite cannot be determined. What is obvious is that, primarily because of lack of prestige, power and money, the brightest students still drifted towards initially into the bureaucracy and later into the NGOs, the corporate sector and the international bureaucracy (UNO, UNDP, World Bank etc). The three defects of the colonial university—subordination to the government, paucity of funds and lack of high academic standards—remained and have even become worse. Let us take them one by one.

Subordination to the Government

As in colonial times, the chancellor is still a high state functionary. For the provincial universities, he is the governor of the province, for the federal ones, the President of Pakistan. The vice chancellor is always his nominee which, in practice, means that the bureaucrats of the ministry of education have a major say in deciding who he or she is to be. While the provincial, or federal, governments exercise administrative control over university affairs, financial control is exercised through the centre that provides funds through the University Grants Commission (now Higher Education Commission or HEC) first established in 1974. In short, government influence has increased since British times because at that time, the only controlling body was the provincial government. Now three separate sets of bureaucrats are involved: the provincial bureaucracy; the federal bureaucracy, and the HEC's bureaucracy. While control has become more diversified and red-tape has multiplied, responsibility has become diffused. In the words of a World Bank report of 1990 that is still valid for most universities:

> This divorce of administrative from financial responsibility means that neither federal, nor provincial, nor university authorities can be held to account for the overall management of the university system. Especially in an environment where tough decisions are required, nothing significant can be accomplished to improve the universities until this duality of management control is ended (World Bank 1990: vol. 1, p. 15).

That is why one finds provincial governments passing orders about increasing student intake in order to please their voters while no new budget to create facilities for the new students is ever given by the federal Ministry of Finance. What these bureaucratic hurdles mean for the faculty is that there is more delay, more humiliation and more frustration. In the past, changes made by the Higher Education Commission, and especially because of the efforts of the Dr Attaur Rahman, a No Objection Certificate was required for all visits abroad. Now they are required only if the visit is for a longer duration. In such cases, an application for funds for research or travel abroad to read a paper in a seminar goes directly from the university's bureaucracy—by itself a major hurdle—to the relevant section of the Ministry of Education. From there it is sent to the HEC that passes it on to the Higher Research Wing. From there it goes to the Ministry of finance and then back to the Ministry of Education that issues the No Objection Certificate for travel abroad when funds are involved and sometimes even when they are not. A self-respecting academic thinks twice before going through this time consuming and humiliating experience. The powerlessness of the academic, which the colonial bureaucracy had ensured, has only increased in the half century of Pakistan's existence.

The University Ordinance of Ayub Khan had suggested that annual confidential reports would be kept on academics; that the vice-chancellors would become much more powerful than before and that academics would generally not elect their colleagues for important offices in the university. Academics opposed it even at that time but with only partial success (GOP 1966: chapter 12. For the demands of the academics see p. 148).

Now the *Report of the Task Force on Improvement of Higher Education in Pakistan* (2002) [subsequently abbreviated as Task Force] has further decrease the power of academics within the university. The vice chancellor will be selected by the board of governors (or senate) and will be responsible to it. However, the chancellor will still be the same as before. These recommendations have been given legal cover in the Model University Ordinance (2002). However, as the Ordinance has not been imposed on most of the universities of the country it is not clear whether academics will really be affected by it as they apprehend.

At the moment, under the old system, the universities are run by the syndicate. In British times, as we have noted earlier, the senate and the syndicate were dominated by high government officials. This has not changed because an average public sector universities' decision-making body has the following officials as ex-officio members:

Table 6.2
Decision-making Body of the Public Universities before the Model University Ordinance 2002

- Vice Chancellor (a nominee of the Chancellor).
- One or more members of the provincial or federal legislature.
- One or more members of the senate.
- High or Supreme Court chief justice.
- Provincial or federal Secretary of the Ministry of Education.
- A nominee of the UGC.
- A religious leader, a woman and two or three eminent people nominated by the Chancellor.

Source: Handbooks of universities.

The only academics are those elected from among professors, assistant professors, lecturers, or associate professors as the case may be. Members nominated by the chancellor, who is always the governor or the president of the country, can hardly be expected not to tow the official line. The ex-officio members are, of course, functionaries of the state. Thus, the voice of the academics is ineffectual even if they choose to take independent stands that under the circumstances, can only be rare. In short, then as far as governmental control is concerned, Pakistani universities still function like their colonial predecessors.

Under the provisions of the MUO the Governing Board (Senate) will have the following members:

- The Chancellor (Chairperson).
- The Vice Chancellor.
- Representative of the government not below the rank of Additional Secretary.
- Four persons from civil society.
- One alumni of the University.
- Two academics not serving in the University (can be college principals).
- Four academics serving in the University.
- One nominee of the Higher Education Commission.

As we can see, this Governing Board is not dominated by academics. In any case, even if it were, the presence of even one or two high functionaries of the state would have ensured the dominance of the latter. Thus, while the MUO may bring about certain improvements, such as the abolition of the NOC for travelling, it will not make the universities autonomous in the real sense of the term.

Ironically enough, Liaquat Ali Khan, the first prime minister of Pakistan, was in favour of giving the faculty more representation in the governance of universities than any government official is nowadays. In the Agra University (Amendment) Bill that came up for consideration on 25 June 1936, he wanted as many teachers on the Senate as possible. Those who opposed him, such as the Raja of Pirpur, demanded more 'public men' rather than academics.

> Liaquat made this expression the object of derision by asking whether by 'public men' are meant those persons 'who are not interested enough to take the trouble of going and canvassing votes to be returned to the University'. The burden of Liaquat's contention was that the Agra University Senate was a legislative body and needed experts. He inquired whether in the Bar Council there should be people other than lawyers, or on the Medical Council people other than physicians (Kazimi 2003: 23).

This is precisely the argument that opponents of the idea that the university should be governed by non-academic people have always made. However, it does not seem to be popular among the upper echelons of the decision-makers of Pakistan.

Paucity of Funds

The colonial universities were poor, though much richer than colonial schools and colleges, as are the Pakistani ones. The total grant for 2002-3 to all public universities is 2974.294 million rupees. Funds actually began to be diverted away from primary education to higher education as a result of change of policy. The year 1987 is used as a benchmark because, as the economist Shahrukh Rafi Khan points out, 'the change in education allocations towards higher education and away from primary education started in 1980-1' (Khan 1991: 211). Indeed, whereas in 1980-1 the universities got 9.94 per cent of the budget on education, from 1987 it rose to 10.88 and stood at 15.19 per cent in 1990. Whether this shift in allocation is justified or not—and Khan argues it is not because it has low social returns and is at the expense of primary schooling (Khan 1991)—the point is that it should have made the universities better. That it has signally failed to do that because much of this money has gone into opening new universities under political pressure. In 1987 there were twenty-two universities in the public sector whereas now, in 2003, there are fifty-three (*Frontier Post* and *News*, 17 March 2003). Out of these, some are white elephants that cost exorbitant amounts to build but are not equipped for standard academic work. The Shah Abdul Latif University in Khairpur, according to Pervez Hoodbhoy, is built with such defective material that nearly thirty buildings were abandoned before they could be used (Hoodbhoy 1997). Money has been lost in these new universities but not in improving the standards of existing ones. All private universities, except the Aga Khan University and the Lahore University of Management Sciences (LUMS), were also established after 1987. The government also gives grants to private universities. According to available figures 12 million rupees were granted to the Aga Khan University between 1991-94 while the share of LUMS in government grants increased by 40.115 per cent during the same period (UGC 1994: 520).

The actual increase in the development budgets of the universities was uneven and not even enough to cover inflation in the 1990s:

Table 6.3
Recurring Budgets of the Public Universities
(in Pakistani Rupees)

Year	Budget of the universities
1978-79	197.133 million
1983-84	469.332 million
1988-89	1090.564 million
1993-94	1527.580 million
1998-99	2083.043 million
2002-3	2974.294 million

Source: Higher Education Commission, March 2003.

Another indicator of the paucity of funds in the universities is cost per student obtained by dividing the recurring expenditure by the total number of students. The following figures are available about this in some of the better known general universities:

Table 6.4
Cost per Student per year in Rupees (Nominal)

University	1985-6	1986-7	1992-3	1996-7	1999-2000	2001-2
Punjab	13,050	14,686	16,745	20,128	19,943	23,399
Sindh	22,279	27,376	18,980	11,986	10,500	27,832
Peshawar	8,623	9,560	11,089	11,315	9,372	17,078
Karachi	10,679	12,182	11,313	20,190	14,904	17,868
Balochistan	14,432	14,503	14,980	13,278	14,982	20,540
QAU	37,430	34,179	34,603	39,682	38,039	40,648

Source: UGC Handbook 1994: 518. Figures for 1999 onwards were supplied by HEC.

If these figures are adjusted for inflation with the 1985-86 figures as the base then the real cost per students is:

Table 6.5
Real Cost per Student per year adjusted for inflation with 1985-86 figures as base

University	1985-6	1986-7	1992-3	1996-7	1999-2000	2001-2
Punjab	13,050	14,242	9,350	7,093	4,657	4,759
Sindh	22,279	26,192	10,597	4,223.5	2,452	5,662
Peshawar	8,623	9,146.5	6,191.5	3,987	2,188	3,474
Karachi	10,679	11,665	6,316.5	7,114	3,480	3,635
Balochistan	14,432	13,875.8	8,364	4,678.8	3,498	4,178
QAU	37,430	32,700	19,320	13,982.8	8,882	8,269

Source: UGC 1987: 518 for 1992-93. Other figures were obtained the HEC. The adjusted figures up to 1996-97 were worked out by Dr Kaiser Bengali and the figures for 1999-2002 were worked out by Dr Eatzaz Ahmad, Professor and Chair, Quaid-i-Azam University, Islamabad both of whose help is gratefully acknowledged.

These figures indicate that, in real terms, all universities have seen a massive decrease in expenditure per student per year.

Still another way of registering the decline in the expenditure on the universities in real terms is to note that the total annual expenditure in 2001-2 was 6.5 billion rupees. The enrollment of all the forty-one degree awarding institutions at that time was 118,000 students. Thus the expenditure per student per year was Rs 55,000. In 1987 it was Rs 20,960. However, in US dollars it was $1213 in 1987 (US$ = Rs 17.39) and $920 in 2001-2 (US$ = Rs 59) (i.e. 25 per cent less than in 1987). Moreover, in 1987 almost 90 per cent of the funding came from the state whereas it was only 50 per cent in 2001-2. This means that government financing is US$450 in 2001-2 compared with US $ 1080 per student in 1987, i.e. there has been a reduction of 62 per cent. The Task Force, like all previous reports, agrees that the total allocation for research is Rs 0.04 billion representing only 1.2 per cent of the total grant from the federal government (Task Force 2002: 14). However, in 2002-3 Rs 3443.393 million was approved for the universities. The HEC is also providing an additional special grant of Rs 520 million for 2003-4 besides money for other improvements. These, however, are ongoing changes which will take time to make a difference.

This failure of the state to support universities has made the universities fall back to generating resources by charging exorbitant tuition fees from students who cannot get admission on merit in the morning session. Such students attend the university in the evening paying much more for the courses than their counterparts in the morning session. The total share of the universities in expenditure has risen from 26 per cent in 1992-93 to 49 per cent in 2000-1. It should be pointed out that the HEC has introduced new schemes for which much funding has been provided in 2004. This would have changed the quality of the public universities if only these were few in number. As it is the money will be spread out too thin and will not bring about the desired improvements. However, it should be pointed out that even in the 'market oriented' universities of the USA, fees are not expected to raise more than 25-30 per cent of the annual costs. The rest has to be met by grants from the state, endorsements by philanthropists, gifts from alumni, research grants and income from property etc.

Lack of High Academic Standards

Pakistani universities lack high academic standards. This is because of the low quality of academics and lack of good laboratories, libraries and other facilities for research. It is also because it is easy to get promoted only on the basis of seniority without doing either good research or teaching. Let us consider some of these factors before moving on to other problems.

Quality of Academics

As in British times, Pakistani universities are staffed by people who are not among the best and the brightest to begin with. A number of high achievers among students, especially middle class ones, are still attracted to the civil service because it gives one the power to manipulate the system for personal gains. Among the gains are illegal ways of obtaining money, favours, and hidden benefits from the state. In a society where even legitimate rights and routine services cannot be obtained without using one's connections (i.e. somebody's influence) or bribing somebody, it is understandable that the young would be attracted to the civil bureaucracy. As for upper class students, or those who are lucky enough to get scholarships, they go to study abroad and generally settle down there and, in any case, their affluent lifestyle can hardly be supported by the salaries offered by the universities. The figures given in Annexure 1 about the income of the faculty of public universities indicate that they mostly (54.33 per cent) fall in the middle class income group (Rs 10,001 to 20,000 per month). About 30.71 per cent, however, fall in the upper middle class (Rs 20,001 to 50,000 per month) bracket. This is not high salary by Pakistani standards since the upper echelons of the military, bureaucracy and the corporate sector earn much higher incomes, (for a comparison see Rahman 1999: Chapter 7).

The following comments about remuneration have been made in many reports:

> Remuneration based on performance, a central motivating factor in most national systems of higher education and research, is an unknown concept in Pakistani higher education. Similarly, for practical purposes, promotions are based entirely on seniority, although in the universities there are also

stated minimum requirements for articles published during the requisite period before promotion can be given (World Bank 1990: vol. 1, p. 16).

The number of required published papers is abysmally low: five to be promoted from assistant professor to associate professor and eight for a full professorship. The UGC (now HEC) does stipulate that these papers should be published in reputable journals but no criterion of the journal is laid down. In practice, then, papers published in newspapers, magazines, and substandard journals are accepted. Most Pakistani academics, even if they are satisfactory as teachers, are not at par with their Western counterparts as scholars and scientists. Those who have made a name for themselves, and there are some who have, achieved this despite the system not because of it. In short, Pakistani academics are generally incompetent as scholars and of indeterminable quality as teachers. However, instead of blaming academics for their lack of scholarly achievement, we should study how the system lets them down and prevents them from becoming scholars.

Other problems that plague the universities are as follows: the system of evaluation is stereotyped, memory-based, corruptible, and stagnant; the universities are often closed because of student unrest; student unions are highly politicized and violent; graduates of universities lack the necessary skills for employment. All of these problems have been addressed by researchers. The problems of the examination system have been recognized since its inception. In India too a large number of reports, beginning with the *Report of the University Education Commission* (1948), have reiterated that it needs major changes (Zachariah 1993). The World Bank Report (1990) and a recent report of the UGC in Pakistan too concern the system of examinations (UGC 1977). After the *National Education Policy* (1979), the semester system (as followed in the USA) was adopted in Pakistan but it failed. At present, the system is followed in the Quaid-i-Azam University, and some departments of other universities. The semester system is not perfect. It forces the students to keep to a narrow focus because some test is always imminent. In the hands of an unfair examiner it is blatantly unfair and, worst of all, it makes students prefer courses in which they can get high marks rather than the academically tougher ones. However, taking just one three-hour examination at the end of year which tests little more than memorization is not a good alternative. In the hands of competent academics, one hopes, all systems would work well.

As for violence on the campus, and the closure of the universities as a consequence, Hafiz Pasha and Ashraf Wasti calculate that it is unacceptably expensive. The students who should have been in the job market lag behind and the time lost can be equated with money lost. Thus a delay of two years in the production of graduates causes a loss of 332 million rupees in social costs (Pasha and Wasti 1993: 17). As for violence on the campus, the World Bank Report takes a position which, though counter-intuitive at first sight, seems to be nearer the truth than the view that if student unions were banned all would be well. This view is:

> ...Campus unrest is probably first and foremost attributable to raging student frustration with the deeply unsatisfactory nature of the educational experience and with the often dubious prospects of suitable employment thereafter. The intrusion of partisan politics into academic life is only an exacerbating factor (World Bank 1990: vol. 1, p.3).

There are many such exacerbating factors and every report on higher education has lamented them.

The most recent report on higher education, *The Task Force Report on Improvement of Higher Education Pakistan* (2002), summed up the views of employers, parents and students in Lahore and Peshawar and all of them agreed that the universities are sub-standard and need improvement. This premise was accepted even by the most persistent critics of the Task Force who disagreed only on the method for making changes and what the changes should be.

The question then, is, what should the changes be and how should they be brought about?

SECTION 3

There are several responses to the crisis in the public universities. The first is that by the private sector and the second by the government.

One response to the failure of the public university system is the mushrooming of the private universities. The first private university was the Aga Khan University established in 1983 and the second was the Lahore University of Management Sciences in 1985. The first taught only medical science and the second business studies. Thus, to begin with, the government of Pakistan allowed one-subject degree awarding institutions to be set up. While both AKU and LUMS kept up their high standards and are expanding into other fields, many other private institutions established later did not. They teach subjects that the market demanded—business, information technology, engineering, medicine, fashion design etc—and charge exorbitantly high fees while providing sub-standard education.

The mushrooming of private universities teaching subjects supposedly leading to lucrative employment is undermining the concept that, among other things, a university education enlightens a person and gives him or her the knowledge to understand the human significance of policies and advances in knowledge. Moreover, the educational apartheid that starts in schools—with the rich and the powerful studying in elitist English medium private schools and cadet colleges—continues in the domain of higher education too. Elitist children, after British O and A Level school examinations, go on to study in private colleges and universities charging high tuition fees, except in the fields of medicine and engineering where those who do not get admission in the public professional institutions go into the private ones. The following figures bring out the difference between the fees of the public and the private universities.

Table 6.6
Expenditure of Students at Quaid-i-Azam University
(in Pakistani rupees)

Tuition Fees	2200	Per semester
Total dues (1st semester)	10,065	Includes tuition fees etc.
Total dues (2nd semester)	4,955	As above
Total dues (3rd semester)	4,955	As above
Total dues (4th semester)	4,955	As above
Expenditure for M.Sc. in two years	24,930	Includes refundables
Average expenditure per month	1,038	As above

Source: Quaid-i-Azam University Administration, March, 2003.

These fees affordable for the families of students in public universities because most of them (more than 60 per cent of them fall in lower middle (Rs 5001-10,000) and middle class (Rs 10,001 to 20,000) income brackets (see Annexure 1).

The fees structure of the private universities is out of the reach of the lower middle classes and even the middle classes. Even the upper middle classes have to sell property in order to teach their children in these expensive institutions. The fee structure is given below:

Table 6.7
Fees Structure of Private Universities

University	Fees (Pak rupees)	Duration	Subject and Level
Al-Khair	100,000	2 Year	MCS/MIT
Baqai	47,500	Per Semester	MBA
	2,27,000	Per Years	MBBS
Greenwich	9,000	Per Course	MBA
Hamdard	8,500	Per Course	MBA
	72,000	Per Years	MBBS
Iqra	12,000	Per Course	MBA
Lahore University of Management Sciences (LUMS)	1,74,000	Per Year	MBA
Aga Khan University	3,92,000	Per Year	MBBS
GIKI (Ghulam Ishaq Khan Institute of Science and Technology)	1,50,000	Per Year	BE

BE= Bachelor of Engineering, MBA= Master of Business Administration, MBBS= Bachelor of Medicine and Bachelor of Surgery, MCS= Master of Computer Science; MIT= Master of Information Technology.
Source: UGC, 2001

Besides the tuition fees, examination, admission and other types of fees also exist in both kinds of universities but, of course, they are far higher in the private sector than in the public sector.

The fact that private colleges and universities are attended by rich young people, who are generally fluent in English and have tremendous self-confidence bordering on arrogance, makes them appear to be 'good' institutions.

The students of private universities come from upper middle class (44.33 per cent) and upper class (17.52 per cent) income brackets who can afford the expenses of these institutions (see Annexure 1). Many military officers and bureaucrats who send their children in these institutions told me that they sell plots of land given to them at cheaper rates by the state in the market where their price goes up several times to pay for this kind of education.

The fact, however, is that the faculty in most private universities is generally part-time rather than full-time and this part-time faculty is from the public sector universities. Except in some universities, such as the Aga Khan University, LUMS and GIKI, the faculty members are not published academics. In some, they do not even have Ph.D. or other research degrees. The classrooms are, generally speaking, air-conditioned and the furniture is better than in the public universities. However, taken as a whole, the private universities charge far more than the quality of education they offer.

Nevertheless, the elitist glitter of the private universities has had the effect of ghettoizing the public universities, like the Urdu medium schools, are increasingly being seen as substandard, poor, incompetent and 'lower class' institutions. In addition, the private universities are generally not governed by academics. They have business people, state functionaries and other powerful members of civil society on their Boards of Governors. Their argument is that such people represent the interests of the corporate sector and the state, the potential employers of the products of the universities, and is, therefore, a necessary development. However useful such an arrangement may be, it does erode the medieval ideas of university governance—that it is the prerogative of academics to govern universities.

Moreover, the idea of the university as a liberal institution where one is exposed to new ideas is also under threat. As mentioned earlier, most private universities, especially those run by the armed forces, are highly regimented and academics have no role in controlling them. Thus, academics, who are called 'teachers' and not 'academics', are treated at par with hired tutors who are supposed to provide a service for payment but have no part in the governance of the institution.

Even worse, the private universities—even those well-endowed—focus on teaching. They require faculty to teach so many hours and evaluate so many students that they do not have enough time for research. Moreover, in most cases, research is not necessary for promotion because of which what little research is needed in the public universities is dispensed with in private institutions.

Response from the Armed Forces

The armed forces have influenced the elitist cadet colleges and public schools by either being part of their Boards of Governors or principals since the 1950s. It is only recently, however, that they have responded to the breakdown of the public university system by creating universities of their own. The armed forces universities functioning at present (2004) are: the National University of Science and Technology (NUST); Bahria University; Air University; National University of Modern Languages (NUML) and the Foundation University. Moreover, the military academies of the three armed forces are also degree-awarding institutions counted among universities by the HEC though in some cases they are affiliated with the armed forces universities. The five major military universities work like other private universities, charging high tuition fees and offering subjects of utilitarian value. They are generally governed, however, by retired military officers. The presence of the military, both retired and serving, is another distinctive feature of these universities. Their Board of Governors, CEOs and officers are given in detail in Annexure 8:

Other details about the military universities are as follows:

Table 6.8

University	Subjects Taught	Tuition Fees (excludes boarding fees)	
NUST	Engineering, medicine, Management, IT, Environmental Engineering	BBA (3 years) IT (4 years Bachelors) Engineering (3-5 year BE) Medicine (5 years MBBS)	2,69,000 2,95,000 2,68,000 4,42,000
		(Wards of armed forces personnel; top scorers and some disadvantaged students get subsidies).	
Bahria	Management, IT, psychology, Naval Sciences, Strategic Studies, Environmental Sciences	MBA MS BBA BS/BTE	2000 per credit hour 2000 per credit hour 1500 per credit hour 1500 per credit hour
		Top scorers are given concessions)	
Air University	Engineering, Management, IT	Bachelors Masters	3,12,000 1,56,000
		(PAF personnel get a discount of 25% in tuition fees).	

(Continued)

NUML	Modern languages, IT, Management, education.		Service personnel are free. There are discounts for armed forces wards in some courses
		Undergraduate courses (Languages)	6965 per semester
		Graduate (Languages)	10,665
		BCS	36,915
		MIT	39,915
		BBA	30,915
		MBA	32,915
		B. Ed	12,265
Foundation University	Medicine, teacher training, business studies.	BBA	37,000 per semester
		MBA	57,000 per semester
		IT	57,000 per semester
		Medicine	2,90,000 per year
		Education	Rs 2000 per month

Source: Offices and brochures of the respective universities.

By all accounts, the military universities are disciplined so that students do not lose academic time in strikes and closures. Most of the teaching is at par, and sometimes better, than that of the same subjects in public universities. They also have well equipped and comfortable class rooms, libraries and laboratories. Their faculty, however, is not as highly published as the faculty of the best public universities (though the public universities do not have highly published academics as noted earlier) (PCST 2004:488).

The number of productive scientists and points (calculated on the basis of publication, citation and supervision of research) are as follows:

Institution	Scientists	Points
Quaid-i-Azam University	68	27,984
University of Karachi	41	10,508
NUST	05	278
Air University	0	0
Bahria	0	0
Foundation	0	0

Source: PCST 2004:488-489.

However, this does not mean that they are not reasonably good teachers. This makes the military universities popular among students who flock to seek admission in them and whose parents pay large sums of money to get them educated there.

Despite all these strong points, the military universities essentially negate the idea of the university as a place created by academics in order to experiment in new ideas. These institutions do not have the air of academic freedom, the bold experimentation with new thoughts and ideas that generally come from independent scholars on the campus, and the air of youthful innovation that characterize campuses like Cambridge, Berkeley and even the larger universities of Pakistan. Moreover, since academics are hired to teach certain subjects and do not govern, they never attain the kind of power and status that Noam Chomsky, Edward Said or Albert Einstein—all three radical in different ways—attained in liberal, civilian, universities. Students who see academics as subordinates tend to respect power rather than knowledge. Moreover, academics themselves develop contempt for themselves. This phenomenon is not new since the bureaucracy has always been dominating academia in Pakistan. What is new is that now, in addition to the bureaucracy, the military too has begun to dominate some sections of the academia. Thus the autonomy and power of academics, such as it was, is being eroded even further.

Response from the Government

The initial response of the government was to increase the number of the universities despite having repeatedly vowed in many education policies not to do so. However, the share of the public sector was to decrease as the private sector was to increase its enrollment from 15 to 40 per cent by 2010. With this in mind, *Education Sector Reforms* (GoP 2002c) declared that a liberal policy towards grant of charter to private universities would be adopted. Moreover, the public sector, too, would be provided with more money to increase its own enrollment (GoP 2002c).

The Task Force is the latest response of the government to the stagnation of the public universities. Formed in 2001, the Task Force submitted its report in January 2002. It met with a lot of criticism because it had recommended a number of changes that threatened to decrease the power of the faculty in governance, increase fees and make tenure uncertain. The concept of governing board (GB), that has been discussed before, has been criticized that it would not increase the power of academics in governing the university and that the vice chancellors could still be bureaucrats or military officers.

The Task Force, however, argues that the university should, in principle, be answerable to the civil society as well as the government—hence the role of members of the civil society and bureaucrats in governance. This idea seems to have been imported from the United States where the Oxbridge tradition was never more than a distant dream of some academics while businessmen called the shots as trustees of universities. As for the increase in fees, the Task Force points out that fee could be increased earlier too. Indeed, now only a 10 per cent increase, and no more, can take place so there is an upper limit on the increase. Tuition fees are, indeed, a problematic issue. In India, the expenditure per year in a typical engineering college in 1992 was US$700 per student per year. In the prestigious Indian Institutes of Technology, however, it was $2500 per student per year. In the UK it was $12,000 and in the USA $20,000 in the same period. Thus the IITs are very cost-effective (Indireson & Nigam 1993: 339).

Considering this, the Pakistani public universities too are very cost effective. However, since quality of education is not as high as it is reputed to be in the IITs, they have to be improved, and increasing fees appears to be an attractive option at first sight. However, it would be a cruel and unjust option keeping in view the dire economic conditions of most of the students who come to the public universities. As for tenure, it is a fact that many of those who oppose it are not productive as scholars. They do not produce much quality research but want a permanent tenure till retirement. In principle, this must come to an end. However, unless the universities are well equipped with good laboratories, libraries and funds for research, it is unjust to expect people to do good research. The HEC, under the dynamic leadership of Dr Attaur Rahman, has provided much more money than ever before in the 2003-4 in the universities. The faculty will be offered bonuses and much higher salaries (Rs 1,34,000 to professors) in the tenure-track system; national distinguished professors have been created in 2004 (each earning Rs 75,000 per month in addition to salary or pension); retired academics as well as academics from abroad are being hired and scholarships, funds for research, travel grants to attend conferences are being provided. These steps will provide incentives to good faculty and may reverse the trend among them to join private sector institutions. However, if the HEC wants good results, all academics, Pakistanis and foreigners, should be given the same emoluments on equal qualifications and work. Above all, the fear is that these reforms will not become a permanent feature of the system of higher education because they are the result of personality (Dr Attaur Rahman) rather than a consensual process at the highest institutional level. The other fear is that being spread out too thin, the money will run out before the reforms are completed.

In short, while the idea of reform is clearly necessary, the modalities of that reform process are debatable. The refore, so some proposals are presented in the last chapter as tentative measures more to serve as a starting point for debate than as final solutions.

CONCLUSION

This chapter suggests that Pakistani universities are sub-standard because the colonial past has left behind a legacy of the over developed state with less money going into higher education than is required. Moreover, because of the prestige and power of the state, academia remains dominated and subservient in this country. Thus, both because of lack of high salaries and lack of power and influence, the brightest minds are not attracted to the academic profession.

Because of the lack of high quality in the public universities as well as the population pressure, private entrepreneurs as well as the armed forces have established their own universities. These institutions range from high academic standards to extremely poor. However, since they cater to the affluent classes they are attractive for young people who are educated in English-medium schools. Thus, the educational apartheid established in schools, that ended at the college level up to the 1980s, now continues throughout a student's career. This development ghettoizes the public university, alienating the affluent classes from the less affluent more markedly than before. It also devalues the significance of the university as an intellectual space where ideas can be expressed freely since private universities generally treat faculty as hired providers of services and not the de facto power holders in the university system. Thus, if the Pakistani university, is to be salvaged then the public university will have to be given an edge over the private university.

This can be accomplished by making the public universities so attractive that the best and the brightest should be attracted to them. This is possible in many ways but all of them require substantial expenditure, determination to take policies to their conclusion and patience to wait for long term results. However, the proposals given by the government in the Task Force seem to increase the role of the business community and powerful members of the civil society without reducing the role of the state in any substantial manner. Some of the reforms introduced by the HEC may also improve the public universities, especially if they are restricted to only a few universities. The proposals suggested in the chapter on recommendations in this book are a departure from the tradition of the colonial university in that they ensure that academics govern universities and that they do become those cherished spaces where the best minds of the country can discuss new ideas without fear.

The College Lecturer's Tale

Adil Hussain (not his real name) had come from the village of Dhok Kala Shah in the central Punjab to the city of Lahore where the lights never went off. In the city, people were up and about even at midnight. He had done well in the village school but the college—and it was a college with a grand reputation in Lahore—almost made him run away in despair. The lecturers actually spoke in English in the classroom. They did switch to Urdu but never to Punjabi—unless they were joking with him—which was his mother tongue. He was used to Urdu, of course, as the masters in the school taught him mostly in Urdu. But whereas the masters explained difficult concepts in Punjabi the college lecturers did so in Urdu. Other boys—and there were at least sixty in the class—seemed to take down notes but he could not make head or tail of what was being said.

Gradually, however, he learned that there were guidebooks that explained things in both Urdu and English. Moreover, some senior boys tutored young students as a favour. He bought and borrowed the guidebooks and found a senior student whose attendant he became. Within a year he knew what was going on. When he had entered the college he loved to 'skip' classes and go out with friends. The school had been like a concentration camp with the masters ready to pounce upon one all the time. But this was heavens itself where, if one walked over to the Mall, one could see girls. One did not, of course, talk to the girls but there they were—wonder of wonders! He also watched movies and sat down in the wayside tea houses where people talked of literature, politics and economics all the time. He listened to them with awe for some were famous figures—people whose names appeared in print and who even appeared on the TV. He too wanted to be like them.

Before he knew it, the intermediate examination came like a tidal wave and he all but drowned. He got a second division though in his matriculation he had first. The medical college was no longer an option but he got admission in B.Sc. This time he was serious but only for six months or so. Then came the drama and the debating competition, and he volunteered for both. He thought it was only a fling but then he got a prize in both and found himself in the college team. The team lived on endless cups of tea and biscuits and one could hardly see through the smoke which the cigarette-puffers created. This was fun! This was life itself!

But the examination was hardly fun, and he had to start his M.Sc. He performed poorly in his dasses because of the drama at which he was an acknowledged master now. He thought he would join the bureaucracy. There was an examination for this too but this time he did badly because his English was still bad. All his acting and debating had been in Urdu but English was still a stumbling block. He failed again.

Out of the college gates and only his village to go to! This was a disgrace. And in any case how could he settle down in the village where his father tilled his own fields even now. He came back to Lahore, stayed with friends in the hostel, and applied for college lectureships. At last, after five attempts, he got one and it was in Lahore itself. When he went home to give the good news to his mother she had news of her own to give him—that he was to be married soon. This was a bit sudden but he knew it would happen some day and so he did not complain.

He lived a life of near penury in a street where lower middle class people lived frustrated but apparently respectable lives. Since nobody took tuitions in biology, there was no extra income of any kind. So, while his friends graduated from bicycles to motor cycles and then to cars, he remained stuck to the same scooter till he retired. With four children, the most he could do was to give them the same kind of education as he himself had received. But his college had become autonomous and its fees had suddenly gone up so that his own sons had to be sent to other places. He had sold his father's land—or what came to his share out of three brothers—and paid for his daughter's marriage. The pension was never enough—and nobody studied biology from him!

The Famous Academic

Qudrat Ullah Khan (not his real name) was the son of a middle-ranking government official in Karachi. He studied in an ordinary Urdu-medium school but he had a radio at home and lived near a book shop that sold both new and used books. He loved to read the books and spent most of his spare time in the shop. The books taught him English and he found college easy. His father forced him into science but he loved history and philosophy. After his intermediate he rebelled and his father, always a kind man, allowed him to take history and philosophy. Now that he was doing what he loved to do, he broke all previous records of the college. With a high first class he entered Karachi University triumphantly and found himself in the History Department.

His family had been conservative and religious but he had read Bertrand Russell and so many Western, liberal intellectuals as to have rebelled against the family tradition. The University too was divided into the Left and the Right camps and he was on the Left. One day, while delivering a fiery speech, he was beaten up by his political opponents. His family was horrified and he did not attend classes for a few weeks. But the trouble blew over and he stood first in the whole university. As the government gave a scholarship to study abroad to those who got a first class with a first position, he got the chance to do his Ph.D. at Cambridge. During his work, he published a number of scholarly articles and was appointed at once as an assistant professor in Pakistan's most prestigious university.

In Cambridge, he had met Aliya who now became his wife. Aliya worked in an NGO while Qudrat worked in the university. Because of his many publications, he had the chance to go for post-doctoral research to the United States, Germany and France. Aliya accompanied him and their children were brought up in many countries. The University did not pay very well despite the fact that he soon became a full professor in National Pay Scale-20. However, he was invited to deliver lectures within the country and abroad and some of the organizations he lectured at paid well. The royalties from his books, all published by prestigious publishers, were not very high but he got much prestige from them. Sometimes NGOs and organizations of the United Nations commissioned research work and paid him extremely well. Aliya too was getting a really good pay package though she was not as famous as her husband was.

When Dr Qudrat reached retirement age he was invited by a private university as a dean. The salary here was much higher than before but he no longer had the time for research. He often said that this was like killing the goose which laid the golden eggs—but then what could he do? Both the daughter and the son were studying in private institutions where the average fees was three lacs (300,000) rupees per year each.

He and Aliya joked that, but for the education of their children, they would have lived like lords. They often wondered if they were not the first generation of Pakistani parents to spend as much money on their children's education as they were doing. And if so, when would the breaking point of such a lopsided society arrive?

7

RECOMMENDATIONS

These recommendations are based on the assumption that the state plans to reform the system of education so that it becomes equitable at the school level and college level (up to BA) and of high academic standard at the university level. This means spending much more money—perhaps three times as much as now—on education than is being done today. The recommendations are for the primary, secondary, college and university education. As for madrassas, any recommendations for change must come from the *ulema* whose views should be respected.

PRIMARY LEVEL (1 TO 5)

Primary schooling should be compulsory for all children all over the country. It should be given in the mother-tongue of the child as far as possible though basic literacy in Urdu and English should also be given. Corporal punishment should be banned and children should be taught through games, films and entertaining songs, stories, jokes in the languages they are taught. Parents should be induced to send their children to the school by giving their children nutritious meals, books, notebooks and some pocket money for incidental expenses.

There should be no elite English-medium primary schools. All children must attend beautifully furnished state-financed primary schools that inculcate respect for the languages of the country in them. In this context Yameema Mitha's school (Muzmun-e-Shauq) is worth mentioning because she, the owner and principal, teaches the children both through Urdu and English. Some teachers are designated Urdu-speaking while others are English-speaking. To give Urdu the prestige it lacks, Yameema Mitha herself is an Urdu-speaking teacher (Mitha Int. 2003). This school is situated in Islamabad and has only forty children. Such a model can be replicated all over the country.

The proposed primary schools should have this model in mind with the difference that teachers will use Pashto, Punjabi, Balochi, Brahvi and Sindhi too in addition to Urdu and a little English.

SECONDARY LEVEL (6 TO 12)

At this level, all schools should continue to teach both in the mother-tongue and Urdu. For this the provinces should be asked whether they would accept Urdu as a link-language. As they practically have, this should not be a problem.

Children's books should make them aware of humanist values—peace, tolerance, human rights, democracy, pluralism etc—and should be well-designed and interesting. They should be shown documentaries on history, the environment, human rights, literary classics and esoteric cultures (from Discovery Channel, National Geographic, History Channel etc.) in English as well as Urdu.

English should be taught, mainly by the interactive method and as a living language, at all levels. However, elite schools with English as a medium of instruction should be discouraged and, when state schools can compete with them and their clientele is reduced, they may be banned altogether but not in a dictatorial manner and not till alternatives are not provided.

COLLEGES AND PRIVATE INSTITUTIONS TEACHING AT THE BACHELOR'S LEVEL

Because of our growing population, colleges and private institutions calling themselves universities but teaching one or two capital-generating subjects will keep expanding. They should be examined and regularly inspected by a Board of Higher Education in every major city of Pakistan—Karachi, Hyderabad, Multan, Bahawalpur, Rawalpindi, Peshawar, D.I. Khan, Quetta, Gilgit—which should provide external examiners, paper-setters and inspectors. All such institutions may call themselves colleges, institutes or even university-colleges. However, they would have to accept such standardization of curricula and evaluation as the Board prescribes. The medium of instruction should be both Urdu and English. Other languages can be used when books and teachers become available.

UNIVERSITIES

The number of public and private universities will have to be reduced drastically to implement the reforms given in this section. No institution that does not have the basic sciences, social sciences and humanities should have the right to call itself a university. In the private sector the only institutions moving in this direction are the Aga Khan University and the Lahore University of Management Sciences. They combine quality with an increasing choice of disciplines and are evolving into universities.

As for the public sector universities, they have many disciplines but neither good libraries nor laboratories. Their faculty is often academically deficient because good students are not attracted to them. If most of the provincial so-called 'universities' are dubbed 'university-colleges', institutes and professional colleges, the remaining few can become excellent universities if the proposals given below are implemented.

SUGGESTED PROPOSALS

Governance

Let us take the different aspects of the university one by one. First, in my view the university must wean itself away from government and develop into an autonomous institution preponderantly governed by academics. There may be two or three members from the judiciary, the corporate sector or the alumni but more than two-thirds of the members of the governing body should be academics from different universities. The Chief Executive Officer (CEO) should also be an academic of the rank of a professor and distinguished as a scholar or a scientist. He or she may either be elected by the professors of the university or selected by members of the Senate. The Chancellor, who should be a symbolic figurehead, should be a famous intellectual, writer, artist or scholar. Most of the decisions on university affairs must be taken by committees. In short, the university should be ruled by committees of academics and not by the CEO or by a hierarchy of officials.

This would be a considerable change from current practices and also the Model University Ordinance (2002), but it will make the universities autonomous and establish, for the first time in Pakistan, the tradition of governance by academia. Such a tradition was established by the Sarkar Committee when it set up the Indian Institute of Technology in 1946. In short, in the IITs the governing bodies do not have officials and ruling politicians as members. However, the President of India has powers as a Visitor of all the IITs (Inderson and Nigam 1993: 335).

One thing that should be emphasized is that the universities should retain their non-hierarchical, democratic character. This means that appointments to the Senate and other decision-making bodies should be on the basis of elections as far as possible. The administrative headship (chair) of the departments and institutes should rotate between the four senior-most academics and the deanship must necessarily be by elections. All major decisions should be by majority of vote in the various committees of the university and the CEO should not have the power of a manager in the corporate sector. Such an atmosphere may appear to be subversive of discipline. It does, however, preserve the independence, self-pride and confidence of academics that is necessary if they are to have the moral courage to express opinions contrary to that of the state or the senior most members of the university itself.

To maintain discipline there should be a university court to which all cases of prolonged absenteeism, moral turpitude and academic fraud should be brought by departmental discipline committees. These departmental committees should comprise three academics which should rotate to give everyone a chance.

Improvement of Faculty

Reforms of any kind in the public universities are resisted because they are imposed from above without due consultations with academics, or (and this cause for concern) because they are not in the interests of the majority of academics. Thus, all attempts to improve the faculty should begin by assuring present faculty members that their present position, terms of service, salary and emoluments etc.

will not be adversely affected. This, indeed, is what the Steering Committee of the Task Force on Higher Education promised. For future I suggest the following:

a. Selection

In order to take the brightest people into academia the following steps are suggested.

(i) Selection for Junior Positions

The present Central Superior Services Examination should be used to weed out the incompetent and select brighter people. Only the top ten students may be allowed to opt for university service.

Most young recruits should, however, comprise those who obtain the first position in their MA examination provided they do not obtain less than an A grade.

(ii) Selection for Senior Positions

The universities should also be free to invite famous scholars and scientists for short, long and permanent tenures from all over the world. Pakistani academics in good Western universities should be attracted to come to Pakistan even if it is for a brief period. In all such cases, the candidate must have a Ph.D. with publications and must have made a recognized impact in his or her field of interest. All academics, Pakistani and foreign, must be given the same salaries commensurate with their academic competence. These salaries must be compatible with those offered in the private sector.

b. Promotion

All appointments in the universities should be temporary unless one rises to the rank of an associate professor or directly joins as an associate professor or above when permanent tenure may be offered. Academic ranks and criteria for promotion are given below:

Entry Qualifications and Promotion

University faculty members must begin their career as teaching/
research assistants. This appointment should be purely temporary and
subject to their successful completion of Ph.D. degree from an
accredited and reputable university in an advanced country. After this
they will be inducted as university lecturers.

Every post will be advertised and anyone qualifying for it, whether
from another university or research institute, will be appointed. The
minimum qualifications expressed in points for each university post
are given in Table 7.1. The points will be explained later.

Table 7.1
Proposed Emoluments and Qualifications for Entry and Promotion of Academics

Rank	Salary	Minimum Qualification
Teaching Assistants	NPS-18 (Status of a major, NPS-18 civil servant).	MA/M.Sc. (first position or among the top ten candidates in the CSSP examination).
Lecturer	NPS-19 (Status of a Lt. Colonel, deputy secretary).	Ph.D. (only from a recognized, highly regarded foreign university till such time that Pakistani universities become equally highly regarded)
Assistant Professor	NPS-20 (office facilities such as computer, phone, shared fax, research assistant when working on a project) (status of a brigadier, federal joint secretary).	100 points
Associate Professor	NPS-21 (computer, phone, shared fax, research assistant when working on a project) (status of a major general, federal additional secretary).	200 points
Professor	Rs 1,00,000 to 1,50,000 per-month + chauffeur driven car + research assistant when	

(Continued)

	required. Status of a Lt. General, federal secretary.	300 points (at least 150 points must be earned from research)
National Distinguished Professor	Rs 1,50,000 to 2,00,000 per-month + chauffeur driven car + office with permanent staff + research assistant. Status of a minister of state.	400 points (at least 300 points must be earned from research)

The Point-Weightage System

In order to create quantifiable criteria for appointment and promotion a point-weightage system is proposed. This means that articles published in indexed journals, courses taught, theses supervised, conferences attended, books published and edited should be given weightage in points. This system is different from the one used to evaluate and rank scientists by the Pakistan Council for Science and Technology, Islamabad (PCST 2004). As the author has no competence in science the PCST system has not been evaluated. The system proposed below is for subjects other than the natural sciences. The new system is as follows:

Publication

Points for researchers in the social sciences/humanities etc.

Every article/paper published in an anonymously refereed, indexed and/or abstracted journal should be given 1 point. For every index the journal is on, up to a maximum of 5 points. Journals not on any index will carry no points.

For example if a journal is on MLA (Modern Language Association Index) it will carry 1 point. If it is on both MLA and Social Science Index, it will carry 2 points and so on.

Books/Monographs etc.

Books published by reputable publishing houses will carry 5 points upon publication. Every positive review in an indexed journal will carry additional 5 points. A positive review in a publication which is not indexed, including newspapers, will carry 1 point.

Monographs, if refereed, will carry 2 points. Each positive review in an indexed journal will carry 1 point while reviews in newspapers etc will carry 0.50 point.

Edited Books/compilations etc.

Edited books and compilations will carry 1 point. Positive reviews in indexed journals will carry 1 point while reviews in newspapers will carry 0.50 point.

Book Reviews

Each book review in an indexed journal will carry 2 points. Reviews published in non-indexed publications will carry 0.50 point each.

Conferences

Presentation of Papers in a National Conference

An invited paper presentation in a national conference will carry 0.50 point. If published in the proceedings of the conference it will carry 1 point.

Presentation of Papers in an International Conference

An invited paper will carry 1 point. A keynote address will carry 2 points. If published the points will be doubled (i.e. paper in proceedings of conference = 2; keynote address in proceedings = 4).

Teaching

Classroom Lecturing

Points for Teachers in All Subjects

Every course taught to students may be evaluated with the consent and prior permission of the lecturer. The evaluation will be on a ten-point scale by students who will not give their names on the evaluation sheet. Any teacher getting less then 50 per cent average will get no points; 50 per cent average will get 1 point while those with 90 per cent average will get 2 points.

All teachers should have the option of not having their courses evaluated by students. In that case they well get no point for their teaching.

Open Lectures

Lectures given before one's peers and public lectures etc may be evaluated with his or her consent and prior permission. The evaluation will be done by the members of the audience on a ten-point scale. Anyone getting below 50 per cent average will get no points. Those with an average of 50 per cent and above will get 1 point while those with 90 per cent average will get 2 points.

All lecturers should have the option of not having their public lectures evaluated by their peers. In that case they will get no points for such lectures.

Supervision of Research

For the supervision of a Ph.D. thesis the supervisor will get 3 points; for an M.Phil. 2 points and for an M.Sc. thesis only one point. However, the Ph.D. thesis should have been sent for opinion to at least three experts on the subject, two of whom should be teaching or doing research in a reputable university in an advanced country.

Supervisors can gain one extra point for every article the student publishes in an indexed, refereed, abstracted journal, provided it is based on the thesis that has been supervised by the supervisor who claims this extra point.

Hypothetical Career Patterns of Academics on the Point-Weightage System

By way of example let us see how the point-weightage system will affect the careers of (1) Researchers (2) Teachers (3) Researchers + Teachers.

Researchers

Suppose a researcher manages to publish two papers per year in journals on five (or more) indices. The points are as follows:
Year 1 $2 \times 5 = 10$ points
In 10 years $10 \times 10 = 100$ points (University Assistant Professor)

In 20 years   200 points (University Associate Professor)
In 30 years   300 points (University Professor)

In short, an excellent researcher, publishing two articles per year in good journals can become a university professor in thirty years.

In any case, the researcher will contribute to conferences, review and write books too. This will result in some outstanding people who will qualify for the highest academic positions in less time. Highly outstanding ones will qualify for becoming national distinguished professors.

Teachers

Let us now take the case of someone who does not publish at all. Let us further assume that the person is a competent, hard working teacher and opts to be evaluated by students who grade him at 90 per cent and above every time. Let us further assume that he/she is teaching four courses per year. Then the cumulative points one:

Years 1	4x2	=	8 points
In 10 years	10x8	=	80 points
In 20 years			160 points
In 30 years			240 points

However, since a person has to obtain 150 points from research, one cannot become a professor if one is not a published scholar or scientist. One can, however, reach the level of associate professor.

Teachers + Researchers

Since faculty members are supposed to do both research and teaching, anyone who is competent in both stands to great advantage. Let us see what the cumulative points for such a person may be:

If the person gets two research publications in good journals and teaches two courses per year, Then, assuming excellent performance in both, the cumulative point-weightage is:

Research journals (2 articles of 5- point each)		= 10 points
Two evaluated courses		= 8 points
Total		= 18 points
In 10 years	18x10	= 180 points
In 20 years		= 360 points
In 30 years		= 540 points

In short, a competent social scientist can qualify for the highest academic positions in thirty years or less by combining research and good teaching.

Scientists

I do not know enough about the sciences to be able to hazard any credible opinion on the subject. A tentative suggestion is that the impact factor may be multiplied by a constant number (let us say 10) to give the point weightage but evaluation of M.Sc. theses and publishing articles with more than three authors should carry no points or very few points. The constant number can be determined by scientists and may even be different from subject to subject.

The income of full professors in good private universities is above rupees 100,000 per month so that it would be realistic and competitive to pay the salaries proposed above and keep raising them according to the market so as to attract the best academics in the public sector.

It is obvious that the system proposed above is so competitive that very few people will rise to the rank of professor. This is how it should be. The rank of professor should become a rare honour, given after outstanding achievement, and there should only be a few professors. Each professorship should be called a 'chair' e.g. Chair in pure Mathematics; Chair in Organic Chemistry; Chair in General Linguistics etc. The chair should have its own staff and funds that will be managed by the incumbent of the chair.

The new system should run parallel with the present system till all the previous faculty retires. Moreover, the system should be put in place only in universities with the potential of becoming outstanding, model, research universities. One may suggest the names of the Quaid-i-Azam University and Karachi University to begin with. After a few years, when brilliant people start getting attracted to the universities, another university may be added to the list.

The measures suggested above would help, but real change will come in only when the power structure also undergoes corresponding changes. The structure we have at the moment, as mentioned earlier, puts a premium on the use of power to extract privilege; the use of influence to obtain gratification and so on. In short, it favours the bureaucracy, the military, the politicians, the businessmen, the feudal lords, but not the good scholars, not the distinguished scientists, not the gifted lecturers.

This kind of power structure is an impediment for the development of the universities in many ways. First, the powerful bureaucracy does not want to reduce its power. Thus, despite all the reports the public has paid for, the hold of the government remains as strong as it was before. Second, the level of spending on the armed forces and the bureaucracy would have to be curtailed and the saving diverted to the universities if they are to be brought up to internationally acceptable standards. Neither the armed forces nor the mandarins of the bureaucracy are prepared to accept this, and third, the bureaucracy, unresponsiveness and corruption of the system make it necessary to possess power or know people who do so. This is the major attraction of the bureaucracy and the military. If the system becomes just, transparent, and impersonal, as Western bureaucracies are in most public dealings, there would be little incentive for bright people to join the bureaucracy. These people would then be available to universities.

However, they would still be attracted to big business that pays more than universities all over the world. This is a problem in Western countries too, but universities do attract people who want enough time to pursue their own agendas of research; enjoy lecturing and interaction with informed peers and students and enjoy the security (after getting tenure) of university professorships. Besides, the universities are prestigious and being part of the faculty of a good university is a badge of distinction. So, for psychological reasons too (i.e. for 'recognition'), distinguished scholars and intellectually inclined young people are attracted to universities. These, then, are the factors that should operate in Pakistan too. Bringing about change in the political system is a tall order. No powerful group can be expected to relinquish its own power. Thus, if changes are to occur, they must come from the pressure of public opinion; in this case the informed opinion of educated Pakistanis. That better institutions, even in the public sector, can be created is suggested by the existence of the Indian Institutes of Technology. In these institutions financial investment is high; the faculty is research-oriented; government representation on decision-making bodies is minimal and there is a sense of pride in the institution (Indireson & Nigam 1993:334-64).

Academic Audit

According to Murray G. Ross, who writes on universities, 'there are many expectations of the role or roles the professor must play in the university' (Ross 1976: 91). They are supposed to be competent teachers, outstanding researchers as well as administrators. In practice, most people are not outstanding in all these areas. However, they must be held responsible to the society and for this purpose an academic audit on the following lines is suggested:

Table 7.2
Proposal for Evaluation of Academics

Rank	Entry Test	Ongoing Evaluation
Teaching Assistants	1. Presentation on a subject of choice	Student Evaluation
	2. Lecture to a class of students—observed and videotaped	Public lectures/ seminars.
Lecturers	1. Presentation on a subject of choice	1. Student evaluation by choice
	2. Lecture to a class of students—observed.	2. Open lectures
		3. Assistance in Research Projects/independent research.
		4. Publications in indexed journals, books, chapters in books etc to shown to a departmental committee of three senior academics and later to the senate of the university if required.
Assistant Professors	1. Presentation on own research	1. Student evaluation by choice.
		2. Citation in journals/books/ theses etc
		3. Invitations to contribute to seminars, conferences etc.
Associate Professors	1. Presentation on own research	1. Student evaluation by choice.

(Continued)

		2. Citation in journals/books/ theses etc.
		3. Invitations to lectures, papers in conferences, seminars etc.
Professors	Inaugural lecture (open to the public with chancellor, CEO and eminent scholars in attendance)	1. Citation in journals/books/ theses etc. 2. Invitations to lectures, papers in conferences, seminars etc. 3. Evaluation of lectures by choice.

In this audit, the focus for the lower academic ranks is on teaching whereas for the higher ones it is on research. Consultancies are not part of the audit as such because, if they have any academic value, they should be published.

Introduction of New Academic Disciplines

The public universities missed the opportunity of introducing new disciplines such as IT, fashion design, environmental studies. This was one reason they lost students to the private sector. Such subjects should be introduced in the public universities. Moreover, the basic sciences, social sciences and humanities should be improved. Some important subjects—linguistics, archaeology, intellectual history, criminology—are not taught in most Pakistani universities. They must be introduced because without teaching a very wide range of subjects, an institution does not deserve to be called a university at all.

Teaching and research at the university level should be mostly in English though Urdu and other languages may be used to make the students comprehend difficult concepts easily.

CONCLUSION

These recommendations require much investment that would have revolutionary consequences by itself. Moreover, they would bring about a revolution in the society because students would study similar sources in schools of the same kind. The elite would meet the plebeians in the school and, hopefully, respect for egalitarianism would be created. Moreover, if all children are provided equal opportunities, we would have a more just society. The madrassas would remain but they would be purely religious seminaries. They would not attract poor children, or at least those poor children who cannot afford ordinary schools, any more.

Our universities will produce original work and won't be merely disseminating knowledge borrowed from the West. If we become a knowledge-producing society, we will be able to prosper in a world that bestows both power and affluence on those with knowledge.

8

CONCLUSION

The brief study on which this book is based tells us something about the system of education but, even more significantly, much more about the system of distribution of resources and power. We find, for instance, that the state's resources are spent much more freely on the education of the elite than of the masses. We also find that the very poor, and those who live away from urban areas, often go without any formal education at all. Then there are the madrassas which absorb quite a large number of the poor and the religious. These are people whom the ruling elite has abandoned though it legitimizes itself in the name of religion and, ironically enough, used them to fight its proxy wars in Kashmir (at least till the reversal of the Kashmir policy by General Musharraf as a consequence of 9/11).

As for the expenditure by the state on the elite the following data helps us understand this:

Table 8.1
Differences in Costs in Major Types of Educational Institutions
(in Pakistani rupees)

Institution	Average cost per student per year	Contributors	Cost to the state
Madrassas	5,714 (includes board and lodging)	Philanthropists + religious organizations	*Rs 1.55 in 2001-2 an additional sum of Rs 28.60 for subsidies on computers, books etc in some *madrassas* in 2003-4.
Urdu-medium Schools	2264.5 (only tuition)	State	2264.5

(*Continued*)

Elite English medium schools	96,000—for 'A' level & 36,000 for other levels (only tuition)	Parents	None reported except subsidized land in some cantonments.
Cadet colleges/public schools	90,061 (tuition and all facilities).	Parents + state (average of 6 cadet colleges + 1 public school	14,171 (average of 5 cadet colleges only)
Public universities	68,000	Parents + state (parents pay an average of Rs 13,000 per year)	55,000
Public Colleges (provincial)	9,572	State + parents (parents pay Rs 1,591 per year on the average).	7,981
			18,756
Public Colleges (federal)	21,281	Parents pay Rs 2,525 for B.A on the average.	

*   The cost per student per year in the madrassas is calculated for all 1,065,277 students reported in 2000. In 2001-2, a sum of Rs 1,654,000 was given by the government to those madrassas which accepted financial help. In 2003-4, Rs 30.45 million will be given in addition for computerization and modernization of textbooks. However, not all students receive this subsidy as their madrassas refuse government help (these figures are from IPS 2002: tables 1.17 and 1.19).

Source: Data obtained from several institutions.

Education, then, is bound with socio-economic class. The educational institutions—elitist English-medium schools, Urdu-medium schools, madrassas, public and private universities are associated with different classes of our society. The rich and the powerful are found in the English schools (private elitist and cadet colleges) as well as the private universities; the lower middle classes and the working (or lower) classes go to the Urdu-medium schools and the public universities; the very poor and rural youth frequent the madrassas. Education does empower and offer chances of transcending one's social class, but not as much as it would in a society where everybody would be educated in exactly the some kind of educational institutions teaching uniform curricula. For the most part, the educational system reinforces the existing class barriers and acts like a devise to close the ranks of the elite (Myers-Scotton 1993). At least, it restricts or makes it difficult for the masses, educated in Urdu (or Sindhi), to master English so competently as to be able to compete with the students of elitist institution who find access to the most lucrative jobs easier.

Moreover, at the lower levels the educational system produces clerks and semi-skilled workers. At the upper level, it creates Westernized people whose lifestyle is dependent on conspicuous consumption of Western products. Both perpetuate capitalism in its worst forms, the lower by providing cheap labour, the upper by creating inane and selfish consumers. Both levels are not capable of ushering in an era of self-sufficiency, egalitarianism and dignity for the masses.

Educational institutions also seem to produce, or reinforce, a certain worldview. These worldviews create identities that make us take an different roles in society. According to Rubina Saigol: *Ref*

> Since people act according to what they know, the knowledge we impart is likely to lead to specific actions. If we create a child full of hate, we will surely invite violence. This kind of pedagogy will certainly be symbolic violence upon the child, and real violence against society (Saigol 2000: 254).

Teaching of hatred

These remarks, although written in the context of critical pedagogy, are equally relevant for the creation of polarized identities identified with religion and secularism in the different educational institutions of Pakistan. One finds, for instance, that madrassa students and teachers are far more militant about Kashmir than are their counterparts in the elitist English-medium institutions. One also finds that the level of tolerance—if treating people as equal citizens is an indicator of that—for non-Muslim minorities and women is much lower in the madrassas than in the Urdu and the English-medium schools. However, university students, even in public universities where they belong to the socially depressed classes, have less militant and more tolerant views. This means that, except in the madrassas where students are not exposed to discourses created in the outside world, the Pakistani educated classes are able to transcend all the militaristic and intolerant values that they encounter in school textbooks, among their teachers, families and sections of the Urdu press.

But this polarization—although between the two extremes of the madrassa and the English-medium—is potentially dangerous. Here are people who live in the same country but are so completely alienated from each other. The madrassa students regard their Westernized counterparts as stooges of the West and possibly as very bad Muslims if not apostates. The Westernized people, in turn, regard their madrassa counterparts as backward, prejudiced, narrow-minded bigots who would put women under a virtual curfew and destroy all the pleasures

Imp

of life as the Taliban did in Afghanistan. The Urdu-medium majority, pulled by these two extremes, sometimes goes in one direction and sometimes in the other. This tug of war continues but it is a battle which nobody can win—if only because victory means the end of diversity and probably a great imposition and injustice to the losing side.

Meanwhile the colleges and universities, where at least the Urdu and the English streams meet and have started to mingle, are also dividing themselves on the apartheid lines of the schools. The private universities (and a few colleges) cater to the rich while the public universities are for the rest. Since the private universities are very expensive the financial burden on the parents of this generation is probably greater than any generation of parents in the history of South Asia. This is probably why the most well paying jobs are increasingly becoming reserved for retired members of the elite—generally the military but also the civilian elite. Both parents work in educated families and the pressure making for corruption is becoming irresistible.

Education is a fast growing industry but it benefits only some entrepreneurs and their hangers-on. It does not produce wealth that can be distributed in society; it increases competition for white collar jobs without, however, increasing their supply in the same proportion; it produces fast growing armies of unemployed youth. Consider that these youths are getting increasingly conscious of disparities in wealth and that, even more dangerously, they have widely different worldviews. Consider again that some of them explain their problems with reference to religion and see the others as being secular and, therefore, the root cause of all their miseries and, of course, the miseries of the nation as a whole. These considerations make one shudder—for these are the ingredients of a class war in the guise of a religious revolution.

There are ways to change this and coercion is the worst one. Initially, what is possible is to improve the public educational system so as to cut the power base of both the madrassas and the elitist English-medium schools. The madrassas will remain as purely theological seminaries and the English-medium schools will shrink before the competition. To tilt the balance against them even further, English itself may be eliminated from both state and private sector jobs within the country. Going a step further, the state itself should stop patronizing English-medium schools since it is a negation of its

Is problem in the educational policies OR their implementation?

own declared policy of providing equal educati[on to]
all citizens. This step would be in line with the spi[rit]
and democratic egalitarianism. The step of ba[n]
should follow from here when it may not be re[...]
Hamoodur Rahman Commission did say someth[ing about]
colleges that, although it has partly been referred to earlier, still needs
reiterating:

> They have not been in existence long enough to enable us to judge the
> quality of their end products, but we cannot help observing that we are
> unable to appreciate the principle upon which such a discrimination is
> sought to be made by the government, particularly in view of the
> constitutional assurance given in paragraph 15 under Right No. VI—to the
> effect that 'all citizens are equal before law'. We are constrained to observe
> that such discriminatory treatment of the schools by the government is not
> justified and that the government should reconsider its position with regard
> to these schools (GoP 1966: 18).

good Reference.

Now, about thirty-eight years later, the state is still discriminating
between its citizens and creating inequality. Moreover, agencies of the
state, such as the armed forces and their welfare organizations, have
extended their hold from schools to colleges and universities where,
among other things, discriminatory fees levels operate for civilians
and armed forces dependents.

good Ref

oppression

The armed forces administer educational institutions in a disciplined
manner that creates the appearance of efficiency and the reality of an
academic year undisturbed by strikes and political disturbances.
Pakistanis value this very much and fully support the handing of elitist
schools (such as cadet colleges) to the military. Since schools are
always regimented even when run by civilians, this argument is not
true for schools. As for colleges, they are administered by civilian
principals but the overall control is with armed forces officers. This is
insulting for the principals and college lecturers who are constrained
to subordinate themselves to military officers rather than their own
senior colleagues. The military universities are also in the hands of
armed forces, retired and serving officers who govern them. This does
not lower academic standards and military universities are popular
with students. What does suffer, and has gone unnoticed so far, is that
military schools tend to militarize young students and that is not
conducive to creating a society that desires peace, values civilian
achievements, believes that civilian supremacy is the basis of liberal

democracy and looks up to academic accomplishment rather than military rank. As for the military universities, they do not allow unusual, often dissident ideas, to flourish which are the major hallmarks of a liberal university. They do not provide the kind of intellectual ferment where students come in contact with the keenest minds of the age because such minds do not like the regimented school-like atmosphere of a military or a regimented private Pakistani university. Another fact, and again one which has gone unnoticed, is that the expansion of private and military universities have further degraded the position of academics. Whereas earlier, despite the forays of the bureaucracy in the highest offices of academia (such as vice chancellors), the dominant idea was that famous academics deserved the highest offices in academic institutions. Now that idea is almost gone as the headships of elitist cadet colleges and now the universities are increasingly going to non-academic people (generally the entrepreneurs). That this should happen is an incalculable loss to academic prestige which makes those who are compelled to stay in academia frustrated and keeps the aspiring first class minds out of this profession.

If the state wants to establish an equal educational system for all its citizens, it will have to dismantle these bastions of privilege. All state-influenced, or state-controlled institutions or institutions administered by the welfare agencies connected with any state department or agency should be governed by the government's own educational authorities and have the same, affordable, fees for all students no matter which sector of society they belong to. Moreover, these institutions too may be governed by teachers (in the case of schools) and academics (in the case of universities) as such institutions are in Britain which is the model we can safely follow in academic governance.

As for the private sector, it will lose its students if English is no longer the medium of instruction and foreign examinations (O' and A' level) are not facilitated by them. Perhaps, at some stage, foreign examinations will have to be banned and even English-medium schools will have to be banned. In any case, if the curricula are uniform,* the private schools will lose more of their clientele. Moreover, till the elitist schools are banned, the government could consider limiting the tuition fees within certain affordable limits (say not more than 10 per cent of declared income of both parents). Other steps could also be contemplated but draconian measures have unintended negative consequences and should be avoided. All these steps will promote justice and remove inequality—at least in the field of education. This may be the first step towards creating a just, egalitarian and democratic society—an aspiration that is fast becoming a necessity in the post-9/11 world.

NOTES

* Barring the provincial language which would, of course, be different in each province (see author's views on the teaching of languages in Rahman 2002: Conclusion; and on reorganization of provinces in Rahman 1996: Conclusion).

1. The quintiles are calculated in Appendix-C of PIHS (2002). They are as under. This income is in Pakistani rupees per month per capita.

1st Q	Rs 620.45 and below
2nd Q	Rs 620.46 – 769.9
3rd Q	Rs 769.1-947.53
4th Q	Rs 947.54-1254.53
5th Q	Rs 1254.54 and above.

2. Ahmedis, also called Mirzais or Qaidianis, are the followers of Mirza Ghualm Ahmed of a village in East Punjab called Qadian. They were declared a non-Muslim minority by the Government of Pakistan in 1974. For their views see Friedmann (1989).

ANNEXURE 1

Monthly Income and Social Mobility of Students and Faculty in Different Educational Institutions in Pakistan

The following information has been collected in response to section 1 of the questionnaire that is given in Annexure 2. These questions are about the income of the family and, in the case of teachers, the medium of instruction of the school that they attended and their children attended.

Section-1: Monthly Income

The figures below give the monthly income of the families of students and faculty as reported by them in our sample. Those who have not written the income, as well as those who have, have been tabulated separately. The correspondence with socio-economic class, is roughly, as follows:

Working (lower) class	=	Upto Rs 5000 per month.
Lower middle class	=	5001 – 10,000
Middle class	=	10,001– 20,000
Upper middle class	=	20,001 – 50,000
Lower upper class	=	50,001 – 100,000
Middle upper class	=	Above 100,000

The income is for the whole family and not of the individuals earning it. In most cases the income of women has not been written presumably because they are housewives and do not get paid. In case their income is written, the family income is calculated by adding their income to the income of the male earning member's income.

Income of the Families of Madrassa Students
N = 142

	Not written	Up to 5,000	5,001-10,000	10,001–20,000	20,001–50,000	50,000-100,000
Pay father	65 of 142 (45.77%)	59 of 77 (76.62%)	10 of 77 (12.98%)	04 of 77 (5.19%)	04 of 77 (5.19%)	Nil
Pay mother	139 of 142 (97.89%)	02 of 3 (66.66%)	1 of 3 (33.33%)	Nil	Nil	Nil
Father and Mother	N.A	1 of 3 (33.33%)	1 of 3 (33.33%)	1 of 3 (33.33%)		

Analysis: Most madrassa students belong to the working classes.

Income of the Families of Madrassa Teachers
N = 27

	Not written	Up to 5,000	5,001-10,000	10,001–20,000	20,001–50,000	50,000-100,000
Pay self	09 of 27 (33.33%)	13 of 18 (72.22%)	03 of 18 (16.66%)	02 of 18 (11.11%)	Nil	Nil
Pay spouse	26 of 27 (96.30%)	01 of 1 (100%)	Nil	Nil	Nil	Nil
Husband and wife	N.A	Nil	01 of 1 (100%)	Nil	Nil	Nil

Analysis: Most madrassa teachers belong to the working classes.

Income of the Families of Elitist English School Faculty
N = 65

	Not written	Up to 5,000	5,001-10,000	10,001–20,000	20,001–50,000	50,000-100,000	Above 100,000
Pay self	11 of 65 (16.92%)	03 of 54 (5.55%)	22 of 54 (40.74%)	18 of 54 (33.33%)	10 of 54 (18.52%)	01 of 54 (1.85%)	Nil
Pay spouse	55 of 65 (84.62%)	Nil	1 of 10 (10%)	6 of 10 (60%)	02 of 10 (20%)	01 of 10 (10%)	Nil
Husband and wife	N.A	Nil	Nil	3 of 10 (30%)	04 of 10 (40%)	02 of 10 (20%)	01 of 10 (10%)

Analysis: Most teachers have written their own income but not of their spouses. They fall between middle and upper middle class brackets. When husband and wife both earn, the family goes up in income even going into the lower upper class.

Income of the Families of Elitist English School Students
N = 116

	Not written	Up to 5,000	5,001-10,000	10,001–20,000	20,001–50,000	50,000-100,000	Above 100,000
Pay father	81 of 116 (69.83%)	Nil	01 of 35 (2.86%)	03 of 35 (8.57%)	18 of 35 (51.43%)	08 of 35 (22.86%)	05 of 35 (14.29%)
Pay mother	101 of 116 (87.07%)	1 of 15 (6.66%)	03 of 15 (20%)	02 of 15 (13.33%)	08 of 15 (53.33%)	1 of 15 (6.66%)	Nil
Father and mother	N.A	1 of 15 (6.66%)	02 of 15 (13.33%)	Nil	04 of 15 (26.66%)	05 of 15 (33.33%)	03 of 15 (20%)

Analysis: Most of them have not written their parents' income. Out of those who have most belong to the upper middle class. More than one third belong to the upper classes.

Income of Families of Urdu-medium School Students
N = 230

	Not written	Up to 5,000	5,001-10,000	10,001–20,000	20,001–50,000	50,000-100,000	Above 100,000
Pay father	95 of 230 (41.31%)	83 of 135 (61.48%)	36 of 135 (26.66%)	13 of 135 (9.63%)	03 of 135 (2.22%)	Nil	Nil
Pay mother	220 of 230 (95.65%)	8 of 10 (80%)	2 of 10 (20%)	Nil	Nil	Nil	Nil
Father and mother	N.A	2 of 10 (20%)	4 of 10 (40%)	4 of 10 (40%)	Nil	Nil	Nil

Analysis: Most have written their fathers' income but not their mothers' who are probably housewives. Out of those of who have written, most belong to working class families. About a quarter, however, also belong to the lower middle classes. Very few are above that in income.

Income of the Families of the Faculty of Urdu-medium Schools
N = 100

	Not written	Up to 5,000	5,001-10,000	10,001–20,000	20,001–50,000	50,000-100,000	Above 100,000
Pay self	6 of 100 (6%)	17 of 94 (18.09%)	62 of 94 (65.96%)	15 of 94 (15.96%)	Nil	Nil	Nil
Pay spouse	82 of 100 (82%)	3 of 18 (16.66%)	06 of 18 (33.33%)	07 of 18 (38.89%)	02 of 18 (11.11%)	Nil	Nil
Husband and wife	N.A	Nil	Nil	09 of 18 (50%)	09 of 18 (50%)	Nil	Nil

Analysis: Most earners have written their income but not that of their spouse. Most
    belong to the lower middle class. Out of the few spouses whose income is
    reported, a fairly large proportion tend to have middle class incomes and a
    very small minority even higher than that.

Income of the families of Public School and Cadet College Students N = 130

	Not written	Up to 5,000	5,001- 10,000	10,001– 20,000	20,001– 50,000	50,000- 100,000	Above 100,000
Pay father	72 of 130 (55.38%)	Nil	5 of 58 (8.62%)	17 of 58 (29.31%)	33 of 58 (56.90%)	3 of 58 (5.17%)	Nil
Pay mother	111 of 130 (85.39%)	2 of 19 (10.53%)	8 of 19 (42.11%)	4 of 19 (21.05%)	5 of 19 (26.32%)	Nil	Nil
Father and mother	N.A	Nil	Nil	4 of 19 (21.05%)	11 of 19 (57.89%)	4 of 19 (21.05%)	Nil

Analysis: Most have written their father's income but not that of their mother. They
    mostly fall in the upper middle class. Very few of them, however, also fall in
    the lower upper classes.

Income of the Faculty of Cadet Colleges/Public Schools N= 51

	Not written	Up to 5,000	5,001- 10,000	10,001– 20,000	20,001– 50,000	50,000- 100,000	Above 100,000
Pay self	1 of 51 (1.96%)	1 of 50 (2%)	17 of 50 (34%)	28 of 50 (56%)	4 of 50 (8%)	Nil	Nil
Pay spouse	45 of 51 (88.24%)	Nil	1 of 6 (16.66%)	5 of 6 (83.33%)	Nil	Nil	Nil
Husband and wife	N.A	Nil	Nil	1 of 6 (16.66%)	5 of 6 (83.33%)	Nil	Nil

Analysis: Most have written their own income but not their wife's. They fall mostly in
    the middle class with families where husband and wife both earn, falling
    mostly in the upper middle class.

Income of the Families of the Faculty of Public Universities
N = 127

	Not written	Upto 5,000	5,001- 10,000	10,001– 20,000	20,001– 50,000	50,000- 100,000	Above 100,000
Pay self	Nil	3 of 127 (2.36%)	16 of 127 (12.60%)	69 of 127 (54.33%)	39 of 127 (30.71%)	Nil	Nil
Pay spouse	106 of 127 (83.47%)	1 of 21 (4.76%)	2 of 21 (9.52%)	14 of 21 (66.66%)	4 of 21 (19.05%)	Nil	Nil
Husband and wife	Nil	Nil	Nil	1 of 21 (4.76%)	13 of 21 (61.90%)	7 of 21 (33.33%)	Nil

Analysis They have reported their own income but most do not report the income of their spouse. They fall in the middle class with more than a quarter, however, falling in the upper middle classes. When husband and wife are both working, the family comes into upper middle and lower upper class income brackets.

Income of the Families of the Faculty of Private Universities
N = 44

	Not written	Upto 5,000	5,001- 10,000	10,001– 20,000	20,001– 50,000	50,000- 100,000	Above 100,000
Pay self	10 of 44 (22.73%)	1 of 34 (2.94%)	14 of 34 (41.18%)	18 of 34 (52.94%)	1 of 34 (2.94%)	Nil	Nil
Pay spouse	41 of 44 (93.18%)	1 of 3 (33.33%)	1 of 3 (33.33%)	1 of 3 (33.33%)	Nil	Nil	Nil
Husband and wife	Nil	Nil	Nil	Nil	3 of 3 (100%)	Nil	Nil

Analysis: Most of them have given their income but not of their spouse. They fall mostly in the upper middle class. However, a large proportion is in middle class income brackets.

Income of the Families of Students of Private Universities
N = 133

	Not written	Upto 5,000	5,001- 10,000	10,001– 20,000	20,001– 50,000	50,000- 100,000	Above 100,000
Pay father	36 of 133 (27.07%)	5 of 97 (5.15%)	6 of 97 (6.19%)	26 of 97 (26.80%)	43 of 97 (44.33%)	12 of 97 (12.37%)	5 of 97 (5.15%)
Pay mother	127 of 133 (95.48%)	Nil	1 of 6 (16.66)	4 of 6 (66.66%)	1 of 6 (16.66%)	Nil	Nil
Father and mother	N.A	Nil	Nil	3 of 6 (50%)	2 of 6 (33.33%)	1 of 6 (16.66%)	Nil

Analysis: Most have written their fathers' income but not their mothers'. They tend to
fall mostly in the upper middle class income bracket, though more of the rest
fall in lower income groups than higher ones.

Income of the Families of Students of Public Universities
N = 206

	Not written	Upto 5,000	5,001- 10,000	10,001- 20,000	20,001- 50,000	50,000- 100,000	Above 100,000
Pay father	27 of 206 (13.11%)	20 of 179 (11.17%)	58 of 179 (32.40%)	54 of 179 (30.17%)	40 of 179 (22.35%)	7 of 179 (3.91%)	Nil
Pay mother	192 of 206 (93.20%)	3 of 14 (21.43%)	7 of 14 (50%)	1 of 14 (7.14%)	3 of 14 (21.43%)	Nil	Nil
Father and mother	N.A	Nil	2 of 14 (14.29%)	3 of 14 (21.43%)	7 of 14 (50%)	1 of 14 (7.14%)	1 of 14 (7.14%)

Analysis: Most have written their fathers' income but not their mothers'. They mostly
fall in the lower middle and middle class income groups. However, about a
quarter of them belong to upper middle class income brackets and very few
even higher. Where both parents earn, the family tends to be upper middle
class in income.

Income of the Families of Students of Govt. Colleges
N = 326

	Not written	Upto 5,000	5,001- 10,000	10,001- 20,000	20,001- 50,000	50,000- 100,000	Above 100,000
Pay father	99 of 326 (30.37%)	50 of 227 (22.03%)	93 of 227 (40.97%)	52 of 227 (22.91%)	27 of 227 (11.89%)	03 of 227 (1.32%)	2 of 227 (0.88%)
Pay mother	307 of 326 (94.17%)	09 of 19 (47.37%)	07 of 19 (36.84%)	03 of 19 (15.79%)	Nil	Nil	Nil
Father and mother	NA	2 of 19 (10.53%)	03 of 19 (15.79%)	09 of 19 (47.37%)	03 of 19 (15.79%)	2 of 19 (10.53%)	Nil

Analysis: Most have written their fathers' income but not their mothers'. They mostly
fall in the lower middle and middle class income groups. However, less than
one eighth of them belong to upper middle class income brackets and very
few even higher. Where both parents earn, the family tends to be middle class
in income.

Income of the Faculty Members of Govt. Colleges
N = 127

	Not written	Upto 5,000	5,001- 10,000	10,001– 20,000	20,001– 50,000	50,000- 100,000	Above 100,000
Pay spouse	93 of 127 (73.23%)	02 of 34 (5.88%)	4 of 34 (11.76%)	18 of 34 (52.94%)	10 of 34 (29.41%)	Nil	Nil
Pay self	6 of 127 (4.72%)	4 of 121 (3.31%)	34. of 121 (28.10%)	54 of 121 (44.63%)	23 of 121 (19.01%)	05 of 121 (4.13%)	1 of 121 (1.65%)
Pay family	NA	Nil	1 of 34 (2.94%)	3 of 34 (8.82%)	23 of 34 (67.65%)	5 of 34 (14.71%)	2 of 34 (5.88%)

Analysis: Most have written their own income but not their spouse's. They mostly fall in the lower middle and middle class income groups. However, less than one quarter of them belong to upper middle class income brackets and very few even higher. Where both husband and wife earn, the family tends to be upper middle class in income.

Section-2: Social Moblity

Social mobility has been measured in the case of teachers. The only indicators that have been taken into account are (a) the medium of instruction of the teachers themselves when they were students and (b) the medium of instruction of their children. As English-medium schools are more expensive than Urdu-or Sindhi medium ones, it is assumed that, when people get relatively prosperous, they tend to educate their children in English-medium schools. It should, however, be noted that a large number of non-elitist English-medium schools charging higher tuition fees than government Urdu-medium schools have started functioning in the last twenty years or so. As a resul, the older teachers in this survey could either go to expensive English-medium schools or government Urdu-medium ones. They did not have the option of attending less expensive English-medium schools that their children have.

Own Medium of Instruction When in School

Institution	Number of respondents	Not reported	Urdu	English
Cadet colleges/ Public schools	51	1 of 51 (1.96%)	31 of 50 (62%)	19 of 50 (38%)
English-medium schools	65	18 of 65 (27.69%)	10 of 47 (21.28%)	37 of 47 (78.72%)
Madrassas*	27	2 of 27 (7.41%)	21 of 25 (84%)	0 of 25 (0%)
Urdu-medium schools	100@	2 of 100 (2%)	88 of 98 (89.80%)	06 of 98 (6.12%)
Govt. colleges	127	5 of 127 (3.94 %)	80 of 122 (65.57%)	42 of 122 (34.43%)
Private universities	44	3 of 44 (6.82%)	16 of 41 (39.02%)	25 of 41 (60.98%)
Public universities	127	3 of 127 (2.36 %)	87 of 124 (70.16%)	37 of 124 (29.84%)

*NB: Out of 25 teachers, 2 (8%) wrote Pashto and 2 (8%) wrote Arabic as their medium of instruction.

Childrens' Medium of Instruction in School

Institution	Number of respondents	Not written	Urdu	English
Cadet colleges	51	21 of 51 (41.18 %)	03 of 30 (10%)	27 of 30 (90%)
English-medium	65	38 of 65 (58.46%)	1 of 27 (3.70%)	26 of 27 (96.30%)
Madrassas	27	12 of 27 (44.44%)	13 of 15 (86.67%)	2 of 15 (13.33%)
Urdu-medium*	100	31 of 100 (31%)	36 of 69 (52.17%)	31 of 69 (44.93%)
Govt. colleges	127	41 of 127 (32.28 %)	19 of 86 (22.09%)	67 of 86 (77.91%)
Private universities	44	26 of 44 (59.09%)	2 of 18 (11.11%)	16 of 18 (88.88%)
Public universities	127	47 of 127 (37%)	26 of 80 (32.5%)	54 of 80 (67.5%)

*NB: The medium of instruction of 1 child (1.16%) and 3 teachers (3.06%) was Sindhi.

Analysis: Upward socio-economic mobility has occurred in the lives of all but madrassa teachers.

ANNEXURE 2

SURVEY 2003

Survey of Schools, Madrassas, Colleges and Universities

Section-1 : Schools and Madrassas

This survey was conducted between December 2002 and April 2003 with the help of two research assistants Imran Farid and Shahid Gondal whom I take this opportunity to thank. The survey was conducted in Islamabad (myself), Rawalpindi (myself), Peshawar (myself), Karachi (myself), Mandi Bahauddin (Shahid Gondal), Lahore, Faisalabad and Multan (Imran Farid). It was a stratified, non-random survey because a complete list of all target institutions was not available. Moreover, we had to restrict ourselves to urban areas because we neither had the time nor the resources to venture into rural ones. The survey was financially supported by the Social Policy and Development Centre (SPDC), Karachi, to which I am very grateful.

Institutions were used as clusters but only students of class 10 and equivalent were given questionnaires in Urdu or English. They were told that, since they were not supposed to give their names, they should not hesitate to give their honest views. After this the questionnaire was read out and explained. The filled questionnaires were collected at the end of the session.

The major strata are (1) Urdu-medium school, (2) elitist English-medium schools (3) Cadet Colleges/Public Schools and (4) madrassas. There is a further stratification between the students and the teachers of these institutions. Gender-wise breakdown is also available. The following chart helps explain these strata:

TEACHERS

	M (ale)	F (emale)	Total
English-medium	18	47	65
Cadet college/public schools	51	Nil	51
Urdu-medium	42	58	100
Madrassas	27	Nil	27
Grand Total			243

STUDENTS

	M (ale)	F (emale)	Total
English-medium	63	53	116
Cadet college/public schools	130	Ni	130
Urdu-medium	123	107	230
Madrassas	142	Nil	142
Grand Total			618

As the views of each strata are taken separately, they do not represent their proportional share in the student population of Pakistan. The ages of the students are as follows:

Institutions	Mean	Mode	Range
Madrassas	19	20	14-27
English-medium schools	14.1	15	13-18
Urdu-medium school	14.4	16	13-20

In the case of the madrassas the range is higher because some of the *sanvia* class groups had older boys who had joined the seminary late. In the O-level groups both 10th and 11th were represented. Urdu-medium schools had only class-10 clusters.

There are two shortcomings: first, the number of madrassa teachers is very low; and secondly, the population of rural areas as well as Balochistan, the interior of Sindh, Northern Areas could not be represented. The first problem is because madrassa teachers were very reluctant to fill in the questionnaires. The second, as already mentioned, is because of lack of time and resources.

Section-2 Universities

This survey was conducted between February and May 2003 with the help of Mr Rao Iqbal, Research Fellow at the Chair on Quaid-i-Azam and Freedom Movement whom I take this opportunity to thank. The survey was conducted in Islamabad and Rawalpindi (myself and Rao Iqbal), Faisalabad, Lahore, Multan, Bahawalpur (Rao Iqbal). It was a stratified, non-random survey because a complete list of all target institutions was not available.

Institutions were used as clusters and students and faculty members were given questionnaires in English. They were told that, since they were not supposed to give their names, they should not hesitate to give their honest views.

The major strata are (1) Public Universities (2) Private Universities. There is a further stratification between the students and the teachers of these institutions. Gender-wise breakdown is also available. The following chart helps explain these strata:

FACULTY

	M (ale)	F (emale)	Total
Private Universities	30	14	44
Public Universities	103	24	127
Grand Total	133	38	171

STUDENTS

	M (ale)	F (emale)	Total
Private Universities	101	32	133
Public Universities	109	97	206
Grand Total	210	129	339

As the views of each strata are taken separately, they do not represent their proportional share in the population of academic and university students in Pakistan. The students of the public universities were those studying for their master's degrees (15 and 16 years of education). Their mean age was 20.6; the mode being 22 and the range being 18 to 35. As some universities allow mature students there is a sprinkling of those of mature years but their numbers are few. The students of private universities are mostly part of the Bachelors degree program (but normally in business, IT or medicine etc). Their mean age is 21.5 years, the mode being 20 and the range being 18 to 40. Here too there are older people, but very few indeed, who may be studying while doing a job somewhere.

The major shortcoming is that females are represented in very low numbers. They are more reluctant to complete questionnaires and also more difficult to access than their male colleagues. Another problem is that women do not work as faculty of private universities; most of them are employed by the public sector and deliver lectures at private universities. Thus, many people were not given questionnaires to fill because they were actually employees of the public sector. This selection made our sample smaller than we would have wished for.

Section 3: Government Colleges

The survey of government college students and faculty members was conducted in May and June 2003 both by Mr Rao Iqbal and me. As there are very few private colleges, and those which do exist are lumped together with private universities, we chose only government colleges for both boys and girls.

The students were studying for their bachelors' degrees (13 and 14 years of education) and their mean age was 19.11; the mode being 19 and the range between 16 to 27 years.

FACULTY

	M (ale)	F (emale)	Total
Govt. colleges	73	54	127

STUDENTS

	M (ale)	F (emale)	Total
Govt. colleges	152	174	326

The questionnaires for students and teachers are reproduced here. Please note that part-2 (on opinions) is exactly the same. Only part-1 is different for both.

QUESTIONNAIRE (FACULTY)

DO NOT WRITE YOUR NAME TO ENSURE SECRECY. WRITE THE NAME of the institution in which you teach with medium of Instruction.

1. Sex　(1) Male　　(2) Female
2. Education: (1) Below BA (2)　BA (3) MA　　(4) M.Phil.　(5) Ph.D.
3. Which subject (s) do you teach?
4. What is the occupation of your spouse Give his or her rank, title, occupational status; salary; grade; income from all sources etc?
5. What is your average total monthly income (write income from all sources such as tuition, publications, consultancies, rent etc.
6. What is the medium of instruction of the school in which your children study (or studied)?
7. What was medium of instruction of the school in which you studied most?

QUESTIONNAIRE (STUDENTS)

DO NOT WRITE YOUR NAME TO ENSURE SECRECY. WRITE THE NAME of your SCHOOL with medium of Instruction.

1. Age
2. Class
3. Sex　(1)　Male　　(2)　Female
4. What is the occupation of your father? Give his rank, title, occupational status; salary; grade; income from all sources etc?

5. What is the occupation of your mother? Give her rank, title, occupational status, salary, grade, income from all sources etc?

PART-II
(for both faculty and students)

What should be Pakistan's priorities?
1. Take Kashmir away from India by an open war?
(1) Yes (2) No   (3) Don't Know
2. Take Kashmir away from India by supporting Jihadi groups to fight with the Indian army?
(1) Yes (2) No   (3) Don't Know
3. Support Kashmir cause through peaceful means only (i.e. no open war or sending Jihadi groups across the line of control?).
(1) Yes (2) No   (3) Don't Know
4. Give equal rights to Ahmedis in all jobs etc?
(1) Yes (2) No   (3) Don't Know
5. Give equal rights to Pakistani Hindus in all jobs etc?
(1) Yes (2) No   (3) Don't Know
6. Give equal rights to Pakistani Christians in all jobs etc?
(1) Yes (2) No   (3) Don't Know
7. Give equal rights to men and women as in Western countries?
(1) Yes (2) No   (3) Don't Know

Section-4: Views of School and Madrassa Students and Teachers

**Militancy and Tolerance Among Urdu-medium School Students
N= 230(Number abbreviated as No. below)**

	Yes		No		Don't Know	
What should be Pakistan's priorities?	No.	%	No	%	No.	%
(1) Take Kashmir away from India by an open war? (abbreviated as open war below	91	39.56	122	53.04	17	7.39
(2) Take Kashmir away form India by supporting Jihadi groups to fight with the India army? (Jihadi groups)	76	33.04	104	45.22	50	21.74

(3) Supporting Kashmir through peaceful means only? (peaceful means)	174	75.65	42	18.26	14	6.09
(4) Give equal rights to Ahmedis (Ahmedis)	108	46.95	85	36.95	37	16.09
(5) Give equal rights to Hindus (Hindus)	109	47.39	98	42.61	23	10.00
(6) Give equal rights to Christians (Christians)	151	65.65	61	26.52	18	7.83
(7) Give equal rights to men and women as in Western countries (women)	173	75.22	40	17.39	17	7.39

Militancy and Tolerance Among Urdu-Medium School Teachers
N= 100(Number= No.)

Abbreviated Questions	Yes		No		Don't Know	
	No.	%	No	%	No.	%
(1) Open War	20	20	70	70	10	10
(2) Jihadi Groups	19	19	68	68	13	13
(3) Peaceful means	85	85	10	10	5	5
(4) Ahmedis	27	27	65	65	8	8
(5) Hindus	37	37	58	58	5	5
(6) Christians	52	52	42	42	6	6
(7) Women	61	61	33	33	6	6

NB:Figures for (3) are uninterpretable because some respondents ticked options (1) and/or (2) while also ticking (3).

Militancy and Tolerance Among Elitist English-medium School Students
N= 116 (Number = No.) (M= 63; F= 53)

Abbreviated Questions	Yes	No	Don't Know			
	No.	%	No.	%	No	%
(1) Open War	30	25.86	75	64.66	11	9.48
(2) Jihadi Groups	26	22.41	70	60.34	20	17.24

(3)	Peaceful means	84	72.41	22	18.97	10	8.62
(4)	Ahmedis	76	65.52	11	9.48	29	25.00
(5)	Hindus	91	78.45	16	13.79	09	7.76
(6)	Christians	97	83.62	10	8.62	9	7.76
(7)	Women	105	90.52	07	6.03	04	3.45

Militancy and Tolerance Among Elitist English-medium School Teachers
N= 65 (Number = No.)(F= 47; M=18)

Abbreviated Questions	Yes		No		Don't Know	
	No.	%	No.	%	No.	%
(1) Open War	17	26.15	42	64.62	6	9.23
(2) Jihadi Groups	25	38.46	33	50.77	7	10.77
(3) Peaceful means	39	60.00	22	33.85	4	6.15
(4) Ahmedis	28	43.07	24	36.92	13	20.00
(5) Hindus	40	61.54	17	26.15	8	12.31
(6) Christians	53	81.54	7	10.77	5	7.69
(7) Women	51	78.46	9	13.85	5	7.69

NB: Figures for (3) are uninterpretable because some respondents ticked opinion (1) and/or (2) while also ticking (3).

Militancy and Tolerance Among Public School/Cadet College Students
N= 130 (Number =No.) (M=130, F=0)

Abbreviated Questions	Yes		No		Don't Know	
	No.	%	No.	%	No.	%
(1) Open War	48	36.92	78	60.00	04	3.08
(2) Jihadi Groups	69	53.08	52	40.00	09	6.92
(3) Peaceful means	73	56.15	48	36.92	09	6.92
(4) Ahmedis	54	41.54	48	36.92	28	21.54
(5) Hindus	84	64.62	41	31.54	05	3.85
(6) Christians	100	76.92	24	18.46	06	4.62
(7) Women	88	67.69	33	25.38	09	6.92

Militancy and Tolerance Among Teachers of Public Schools/Cadet Colleges
N= 51 (Number = No.)(M= 51; F=0)

Abbreviated Questions	Yes		No		Don't Know	
	No.	%	No.	%	No.	%
(1) Open War	10	19.61	35	68.63	06	11.76
(2) Jihadi Groups	20	39.22	27	52.94	04	7.84
(3) Peaceful means	34	66.66	10	19.61	07	13.73
(4) Ahmedis	15	29.41	32	62.75	04	7.84
(5) Hindus	31	60.78	18	35.29	02	3.92
(6) Christians	31	60.78	17	33.33	03	5.88
(7) Women	19	37.25	30	58.82	02	3.92

Militancy and Tolerance Among Madrassa Students
N= 142 (Number =No.) (M=142, F=0)

Abbreviated Questions	Yes		No		Don't Know	
	No.	%	No.	%	No.	%
(1) Open War	85	59.86	45	31.69	12	8.45
(2) Jihadi Groups	75	52.82	46	32.39	21	14.79
(3) Peaceful means	48	33.80	78	54.93	16	11.27
(4) Ahmedis	18	12.68	117	82.39	7	4.93
(5) Hindus	24	16.90	108	76.06	10	7.04
(6) Christians	26	18.31	104	73.24	12	8.45
(7) Women	24	16.90	110	77.46	8	5.63

Militancy and Tolerance Among Madrassa Teachers
N= 27 (Number = No.)(M= 27; F=0)

Abbreviated Questions	Yes		No		Don't Know	
	No.	%	No.	%	No.	%
(1) Open War	19	70.37	6	22.22	2	7.41
(2) Jihadi Groups	16	59.26	8	29.63	3	11.11

(3) Peaceful means	8	29.63	18	66.67	1	3.70
(4) Ahmedis	1	3.70	26	96.30	Nil	Nil
(5) Hindus	4	14.81	23	85.19	Nil	Nil
(6) Christians	5	18.52	21	77.77	1	3.70
(7) Women	1	3.70	26	96.30	Nil	Nil

NB: Figures for (3) are uninterpretable because some respondents ticked opinion (1) and/or (2) while also ticking (3).

Section-5: Views of University Students and Faculty Militancy and Tolerance Among Public University Students N= 206 (Number abbreviated as No. below)

What should be Pakistan's priorities?	Yes No.	%	No No	%	Don't Know No.	%
(1) Take Kashmir away from India by an open war? (abbreviated as open war below)	72	34.95	114	55.34	20	9.71
(2) Take Kashmir away form India by supporting Jihadi groups to fight with the India army? (Jihadi groups)	95	46.12	89	43.20	22	10.68
(3) Supporting Kashmir through peaceful means only? (peaceful means)	120	58.25	59	28.64	27	13.11
(4) Give equal rights to Ahmedis (Ahmedis)	80	38.83	102	49.51	24	11.65
(5) Give equal rights to Hindus (Hindus)	112	54.37	80	38.83	14	6.80
(6) Give equal rights to Christians (Christians)	138	66.99	60	29.13	8	3.88
(7) Give equal rights to men and women as in Western countries (women)	133	64.56	65	31.55	8	3.88

Militancy and Tolerance Among Public University Academics
N= 127 (Number= No.) M=103, F=24

Abbreviated Questions	Yes		No		Don't Know	
	No.	%	No	%	No.	%
(1) Open War	18	14.17	98	77.17	11	8.66
(2) Jihadi Groups	33	25.98	80	62.99	14	11.02
(3) Peaceful means	96	75.59	23	18.11	8	6.30
(4) Ahmedis	64	50.39	44	34.65	19	14.96
(5) Hindus	84	66.14	33	25.98	10	7.87
(6) Christians	87	68.50	31	24.41	9	7.09
(7) Women	91	71.65	28	22.05	8	6.30

NB Figures for (3) are uninterpretable because some respondents ticked options (1) and/or (2) while also ticking (3).

Militancy and Tolerance Among Private University Students
N= 133 (Number = No.) (M= 101; F= 32)

Abbreviated Questions	Yes		No		Don't Know	
	No.	%	No.	%	No	%
(1) Open War	47	35.34	77	57.89	9	6.77
(2) Jihadi Groups	46	34.59	76	57.14	11	8.27
(3) Peaceful means	76	57.14	47	35.34	10	7.52
(4) Ahmedis	54	40.60	49	36.84	30	22.56
(5) Hindus	93	69.92	28	21.05	12	9.02
(6) Christians	105	78.95	19	14.29	9	6.77
(7) Women	102	76.69	23	17.29	8	6.02

Militancy and Tolerance Among Private University Academics
N= 44 (Number = No.)(F= 14; M=30)

Abbreviated Questions	Yes		No		Don't Know	
	No.	%	No.	%	No.	%
(1) Open War	9	20.45	28	63.64	7	15.91
(2) Jihadi Groups	15	34.09	20	45.45	9	20.45

(3)	Peaceful means	30	68.18	8	18.18	6	13.64
(4)	Ahmedis	26	59.09	13	29.55	5	11.36
(5)	Hindus	30	68.18	10	22.73	4	9.09
(6)	Christians	33	75.00	7	15.91	4	9.09
(7)	Women	35	79.55	7	15.91	2	4.55

NB: Figures for (3) are uninterpretable because some respondents ticked opinion (1) and/or (2) while also ticking (3).

Section. 6: Views of Govt. College Students and Faculty.

Militancy and Tolerance Among Govt. College Students
N= 326 (Number = No.)(F= 174; M=152)

Abbreviated Questions		Yes	No		Don't Know		
		No.	%	No.	%	No.	%
(1)	Open War	150	46.01	158	48.47	18	5.52
(2)	Jihadi Groups	163	50	124	38.04	39	11.96
(3)	Peaceful means	197	60.43	74	22.70	55	16.87
(4)	Ahmedis	124	38.04	125	38.34	77	23.62
(5)	Hindus	193	59.20	104	31.90	29	8.89
(6)	Christians	235	72.09	69	21.17	22	6.75
(7)	Women	213	65.34	101	30.98	12	3.68

Militancy and Tolerance Among Govt. College Faculty
N= 127 (Number = No.) (F= 54; M=73)

Abbreviated Questions		Yes	No		Don't Know		
		No.	%	No.	%	No.	%
(1)	Open War	26	20.47	87	68.50	14	11.02
(2)	Jihadi Groups	23	18.11	81	63.78	23	18.11
(3)	Peaceful means	98	77.17	17	13.39	12	9.45
(4)	Ahmedis	41	32.28	67	52.76	19	14.96
(5)	Hindus	53	41.73	61	48.03	13	10.24
(6)	Christians	75	59.06	41	32.28	11	8.66
(7)	Women	84	66.14	39	30.71	4	3.15

Consolidated Data of Opinions Indicating Militancy and Tolerance Among Three Types of Schools Students in Pakistan in Survey 2003 (in percentages)

Abbreviated Questions		Madrassas (142)	Urdu-medium (230)	English-medium (116)	Cadet Colleges/Public Schools (130)	Govt. Colleges (326)	Public Universities (206)	Private Universities (133)
1. Open War	Yes	59.86	39.56	25.86	36.92	46.01	34.95	35.34
	No	31.69	53.04	64.66	60.00	48.47	55.34	57.89
	Don't Know	8.45	7.39	9.48	3.08	5.52	9.71	6.77
2. Jihadi groups	Yes	52.82	33.04	22.41	53.08	50.00	46.12	34.59
	No	32.39	45.22	60.34	40.00	38.04	43.20	57.14
	Don't Know	14.79	21.74	17.24	6.92	11.96	10.68	8.27
3. Peaceful means	Yes	33.80	75.65	72.41	56.15	60.43	58.25	57.14
	No	54.93	18.26	18.97	36.92	22.70	28.64	35.34
	Don't Know	11.27	6.09	8.62	6.92	16.87	13.11	7.52
4. Ahmedis	Yes	12.68	46.95	65.52	41.54	38.04	38.83	40.60
	No	82.39	36.95	9.48	36.92	38.34	49.51	36.84
	Don't Know	4.93	16.09	25.00	21.54	23.62	11.65	22.56
5. Hindus	Yes	16.90	47.39	78.45	64.62	59.20	54.37	69.92
	No	76.06	42.61	13.79	31.54	31.90	38.83	21.05
	Don't Know	7.04	10.00	7.76	3.85	8.89	6.80	9.02
6. Christians	Yes	18.31	65.65	83.62	76.92	72.09	66.99	78.95
	No	73.24	26.52	8.62	18.46	21.17	29.13	14.29
	Don't Know	8.45	7.83	7.76	4.62	6.75	3.88	6.77
7. Women	Yes	16.90	75.22	90.52	67.69	65.34	64.56	76.69
	No	77.46	17.39	6.03	25.38	30.98	31.55	17.29
	Don't Know	5.63	7.39	3.45	6.92	3.68	3.88	6.02

NB: Figures for (3) are uninterpretable because some respondents ticked opinion (1) and/or (2) while also ticking (3).

Comparative Chart for Opinions of Faculty Members of Different Educational Institutions (percentages)

		Madrassas (27)	Urdu-medium schools (100)	English-medium schools (65)	Cadet Colleges/Public Schools (51)	Govt. Colleges (127)	Private Universities (44)	Public Universities (127)
1. Open War	Yes	70.37	20	26.15	19.61	20.47	20.45	14.17
	No	22.22	70	64.62	68.63	68.50	63.64	77.17
	Don't Know	7.41	10	9.23	11.76	11.02	15.91	8.66
2. Jihadi groups	Yes	59.26	19	38.46	39.22	18.11	34.09	25.98
	No	29.63	68	50.77	52.94	63.78	45.45	62.99
	Don't Know	11.11	13	10.77	7.84	18.11	20.45	11.02
3. Peaceful means	Yes	29.63	85	60.00	66.66	77.17	68.18	75.59
	No	66.67	10	33.85	19.61	13.39	18.18	18.11
	Don't Know	3.70	5	6.15	13.73	9.45	13.64	6.30
4. Ahmedis	Yes	3.70	27	43.07	29.41	32.28	59.09	50.39
	No	96.30	65	36.92	62.75	52.76	29.55	34.65
	Don't Know	NIL	8	20.00	7.84	14.96	11.36	14.96
5. Hindus	Yes	14.81	37	61.54	60.78	41.73	68.18	66.14
	No	85.19	58	26.15	35.29	48.03	22.73	25.98
	Don't Know	NIL	5	12.31	3.92	10.24	9.09	7.87
6. Christians	Yes	18.52	52	81.54	60.78	59.06	75.00	68.50
	No	77.77	42	10.77	33.33	32.28	15.91	24.41
	Don't Know	3.70	6	7.69	5.88	8.66	9.09	7.09
7. Women	Yes	3.70	61	78.46	37.25	66.14	79.55	71.65
	No	96.30	33	13.85	58.82	30.71	15.91	22.05
	Don't Know	NIL	6	7.69	3.92	3.15	4.55	6.30

ANNEXURE 2.1

Gender-Wise Survey of the Opinions of the Students and Faculty of Educational Institutions in Pakistan

Section-1: Schools

ENGLISH MEDIUM ELITIST SCHOOLS

	Students	Teachers
Males	63	18
Females	53	47
Total	116	65

URDU MEDIUM SCHOOLS

	Students	Teachers
Males	123	42
Females	107	58
Total	230	100

Tolerance Among Students of English Medium Schools
N=116 (M=63; F=53)
(In percentages)

Q-4. Give equal rights to *Ahmedis* in all jobs etc?

	Males	Females
Yes	67.74	63.46
No	8.06	11.54
Don't know	24.19	25.00

Q-5.Give equal rights to Pakistani Hindus in all jobs etc?

Yes	75.81	80.77
No	14.52	13.46
Don't know	9.68	5.77

Q-6. Give equal rights to Pakistani Christians in all jobs etc?

Yes	87.09	78.85
No	4.84	13.46
Don't know	8.06	7.69

Q-7. Give equal rights to men and women as in western countries?

Yes	85.48	96.15
No	8.06	3.85
Don't know	6.45	Nil

Analysis: Boys are slightly more tolerant of Ahmedis and Christians than girls. As expected, girls favour equal rights for men and women.

Militancy Among Students of English-Medium Schools
N=116 (M=63; F=53)

What should be Pakistan's priorities?

Q-1 Take Kashmir away from India by an open war?

	Males	Females
Yes	24.02	28.08
No	69.04	59.06
Don't know	6.05	11.05

Q-2 Take Kashmir away from India by supporting Jihadi groups to fight with the Indian army?

Yes	22.58	23.07
No	72.58	44.23
Don't know	4.84	32.69

Q-3 Support Kashmir cause through peaceful means only (i.e. no open war or sending Jihadi groups across the line of control?

Yes	67.74	76.92
No	24.19	13.46
Don't know	8.06	9.62

Analysis Girls have a slightly greater desire than boys for a peaceful solution to the Kashmir problem. However, they are confused about sending fighters across the LOC. As some students ticked Q.3 as well as Q.1 or/and Q.2, the results are uncertain.

Militancy Among English-Medium School Teachers
N=65 (M=18, F=47)
(In percentages)

		Males	Females
Q-1 Kashmir War	Yes	22.22	27.66
	No	72.22	61.70
	Don't know	5.55	10.64
Q-2 Kashmir Jihad	Yes	38.88	38.29
	No	50.00	51.06
	Don't know	11.11	10.64
Q-3 Kashmir Peace	Yes	61.11	59.57
	No	22.22	38.29
	Don't know	16.66	2.13

Analysis: Female teachers appear to favour militant policies in Kashmir slightly more than their male colleagues.

Tolerance Among English-Medium School Teachers
N=65 (M=18, F=47)
(In percentages)

		Males	Females
Ahmedis	Yes	38.88	59.57
	No	22.22	38.29
	Don't know	16.66	2.13
Hindus	Yes	88.88	51.06
	No	Nil	36.17

	Don't know	11.11	12.76
Christians	Yes	88.88	78.72
	No	Nil	14.89
	Don't know	11.11	6.38
Women	Yes	66.66	82.98
	No	22.22	10.64
	Don't know	11.11	6.38

Analysis: Female teachers are less tolerant than their male colleagues for Hindus and Christians. However, they support equal rights for Ahmedis more than males. As expected, they are much more supportive of equal rights for males and females than men.

Militancy Among Urdu-Medium School Students
N=230 out of which M=123 and F=107
(In percentages)

		Males	Females
Kashmir War	Yes	45.53	32.71
	No	49.59	57.01
	Don't know	4.88	10.28
Kashmir Jihad	Yes	38.21	26.17
	No	39.02	57.01
	Don't know	21.95	10.28
Kashmir Peace	Yes	68.29	84.11
	No	23.57	12.15
	Don't know	21.95	3.74

Analysis: Male students are more supportive of militant policies about Kashmir than females. Results for Q.3 are confused because students ticked 'Yes' in response to Q.1 and/or Q.2 while also ticking 'Yes' in Q.3.

Tolerance Among Urdu-Medium School Students
N=230 (M=123 and F=107)
(In percentages)

		Males	Females
1. Ahmedis	Yes	44.71	49.53
	No	39.02	34.58
	Don't know	16.26	15.89
2. Hindus	Yes	51.22	42.99
	No	39.84	44.86
	Don't know	8.13	12.15
3. Christians	Yes	64.23	67.29
	No	27.64	25.23
	Don't know	7.32	7.84
4. Women	Yes	67.48	84.11
	No	21.95	12.15
	Don't Know	9.76	3.74

Analysis: Females are somewhat more tolerant of religious minorities than males. However, in the case of Hindus the males tend to be more tolerant. As for equal rights for men and women, girls favour it significantly more than boys.

Militancy Among Urdu-Medium Teachers
N=100 (M=42 and F=58)
(In percentages)

		Males	Females
1. Kashmir War	Yes	30.95	12.06
	No	57.14	79.31
	Don't know	11.90	8.63
2. Kashmir Jihad	Yes	30.95	10.34
	No	50.00	81.03
	Don't know	19.05	8.62
3. Kashmir Peace	Yes	76.19	91.38
	No	14.29	6.89
	Don't know	9.52	1.72

Analysis:Males support militant policies regarding Kashmir far more than females.

Tolerance Among Urdu-Medium School Teachers
N=100 (M=42 and F=58)
(In percentages)

		Males	Females
1. Ahmedis	Yes	26.19	27.59
	No	66.66	63.79
	Don't know	7.14	8.62
2. Hindus	Yes	40.48	34.48
	No	54.76	60.34
	Don't know	4.76	5.17
3. Christians	Yes	45.24	56.87
	No	47.62	37.93
	Don't know	7.14	5.17
4. Women	Yes	35.71	79.31
	No	54.76	17.24
	Don't Know	9.52	3.45

Analysis: Females are somewhat more tolerant about religious minorities than men. However, in the case of Hindus they are more intolerant than the latter. As for equality of the rights of men and women, men oppose it while women support it vehemently.

Section-2: Colleges

	Govt. Colleges	
	Students	Teachers
Males	152	73
Females	174	54
Total	326	127

Militancy and Tolerance Among College Faculty
N=127 (M=73 and F=54)
(In percentages)

		Males	Females
1. Kashmir War	Yes	19.18	22.22
	No	67.12	70.37
	Don't know	13.70	7.41
2. Kashmir Jihad	Yes	17.81	18.52
	No	61.64	66.66
	Don't know	20.55	14.81
3. Kashmir Peace	Yes	78.08	75.93
	No	10.96	16.66
	Don't know	10.96	7.41
4. Ahmedis	Yes	34.25	29.63
	No	47.95	59.26
	Don't know	17.81	11.11
5. Hindus	Yes	43.84	38.88
	No	45.21	51.85
	Don't know	10.96	9.26
6. Christians	Yes	54.69	64.81
	No	34.25	29.63
	Don't know	10.96	5.55
7. Women	Yes	61.64	72.22
	No	35.62	24.07
	Don't know	2.74	3.70

Analysis: Both men and women and not supportive of militancy. However, they are not
   tolerant of Ahmedis and Hindus. Women are, however, more tolerant of
   Christians than men and far more tolerant of equal rights of women than their
   male colleagues.

Militancy and Tolerance Among College Students
N=326 (M=152 and F=174)
(In percentages)

		Males	Females
1. Kashmir War	Yes	41.45	50.00
	No	55.26	42.53
	Don't know	3.29	7.47
2. Kashmir Jihad	Yes	50.00	50.00
	No	42.76	33.91
	Don't know	7.24	16.09
3. Kashmir Peace	Yes	61.18	59.77
	No	30.92	15.52
	Don't know	7.89	24.71
4. Ahmedis	Yes	36.18	39.66
	No	43.42	33.91
	Don't know	20.39	26.44
5. Hindus	Yes	61.84	56.90
	No	26.32	36.78
	Don't know	11.84	6.32
6. Christians	Yes	67.11	76.44
	No	23.68	18.97
	Don't know	9.21	4.60
7. Women	Yes	55.92	73.56
	No	42.11	21.26
	Don't know	1.97	5.17

Analysis: Females are somewhat more supportive of militant policies than males. However, they are slightly more tolerant towards Ahmedis and Christians than males. They are far more supportive of equal rights for women than their male counterparts.

Section-3: Universities

Public Universities		
	Students	Teachers
Males	109	103
Females	97	24
Total	206	127

Private Universities		
	Students	Teachers
Males	101	30
Females	32	14
Total	133	44

Militancy and Tolerance Among Private University Faculty
N=44 (M=30 and F=14)
(In percentages)

		Males	Females
1. Kashmir War	Yes	23.33	14.29
	No	63.33	64.29
	Don't know	13.33	21.43
2. Kashmir Jihad	Yes	36.66	28.57
	No	43.33	50
	Don't know	20	21.43
3. Kashmir Peace	Yes	63.33	78.57
	No	23.33	7.14
	Don't know	13.33	14.29
4. Ahmedis	Yes	60	57.14
	No	30	28.57
	Don't know	10	14.29
5. Hindus	Yes	70	64.29

	No	23.33	21.43
	Don't know	6.66	14.29
6. Christians	Yes	73.33	78.57
	No	16.66	14.29
	Don't know	10	7.14
7. Women	Yes	73.33	92.86
	No	20	7.14
	Don't know	6.66	Nil

Analysis: Men are more militant but slightly more tolerant of religious minorities except Christians than women. However, women support equal rights for women much more strongly than their male colleagues. This data is not reliable because the number of women, as well as men, who agreed to answer the questionnaires were very few.

Militancy and Tolerance Among Private University Students
N=133(M=101 and F=32)
(In percentages)

		Males	Females
1. Kashmir War	Yes	36.63	31.25
	No	56.44	62.50
	Don't know	6.93	6.25
2. Kashmir Jihad	Yes	35.64	31.25
	No	55.45	62.50
	Don't know	8.91	6.25
3. Kashmir Peace	Yes	54.46	65.63
	No	38.61	25.00
	Don't know	6.93	9.34
4. Ahmedis	Yes	35.64	56.25
	No	42.57	18.75
	Don't know	21.78	25.00
5. Hindus	Yes	77.23	62.50
	No	19.80	25.00
	Don't know	7.92	12.50
6. Christians	Yes	78.22	81.25

	No	16.83	6.25
	Don't know	4.95	12.50
7. Women	Yes	72.28	90.63
	No	19.80	9.38
	Don't know	7.92	Nil

Analysis: Females were less militant and more tolerant of religious minorities, except
Hindus, than males. They were much more supportive of equal rights for
women than their male counterparts.

Militancy and Tolerance Among Public University Students
(M=109 and F=97)
(In percentages)

		Males	Females
1. Kashmir War	Yes	35.78	34.02
	No	56.88	53.61
	Don't know	7.34	12.37
2. Kashmir Jihad	Yes	52.29	39.16
	No	40.37	46.39
	Don't know	7.34	14.43
3. Kashmir Peace	Yes	56.88	59.79
	No	33.94	22.68
	Don't know	9.17	17.53
4. Ahmedis	Yes	32.11	46.39
	No	58.72	39.18
	Don't know	9.17	14.43
5. Hindus	Yes	55.96	52.58
	No	38.53	39.18
	Don't know	5.50	8.25
6. Christians	Yes	65.14	69.07
	No	32.11	25.77
	Don't know	2.75	5.15
7. Women	Yes	52.29	78.35

No		44.03	17.53
Don't know		3.67	4.12

Analysis: Females are less militant than males. They are also more supportive of
religious minorities except Hindus. They are much more supportive of equal
rights for women than their male counterparts.

Militancy and Tolerance Among Public University Faculty
N= 127(M=103 and F=24)
(In percentages)

		Males	Females
1. Kashmir War	Yes	15.53	8.33
	No	73.79	91.66
	Don't know	10.68	Nil
2. Kashmir Jihad	Yes	25.24	29.17
	No	61.17	70.83
	Don't know	13.59	Nil
3. Kashmir Peace	Yes	73.79	83.33
	No	19.42	12.5
	Don't know	6.80	4.17
4. Ahmedis	Yes	49.51	54.17
	No	36.89	25
	Don't know	13.59	20.83
5. Hindus	Yes	64.08	75
	No	28.16	16.67
	Don't know	7.77	8.33
6. Christians	Yes	66.99	75
	No	27.18	12.5
	Don't know	5.83	12.5
7. Women	Yes	66.99	91.66
	No	25.24	8.33
	Don't know	7.77	Nil

Analysis: Females are far less militant and far more supportive of equal rights for
minorities and women than their male counterparts. However, since only 24
women agreed to fill in the questionnaires the data on women may be
unrepresentative of the population.

ANNEXURE 3

Matriculation Examination (2002)
Board of Intermediate & Secondary Education, Rawalpindi

Budget	Pass percentage
Overall	50 (87,064 candidates)
English	67
Urdu	90
Pakistan Studies	83
Islamic Studies	90
Mathematics	62

NB: These are the results of compulsory subjects. In optional ones too, English comes among subjects where the passing rate is low.

Source: Board of Intermediate & Secondary Education, Rawalpindi.

ANNEXURE 4

NUMBER OF MADRASSAS

The Government of Pakistan's report on the madrassas (GoP 1988) has given the number of madrassas in every province and other parts of Pakistan. The report, along with the increase in recent years, is being reproduced here. However, the numbers in each province is not available in recent sources. Thus the numbers for 2002 are based on many sources and do not give a reliable picture for all provinces.

Area	Others/ Jamat		Deobandi		Barelvi@		Ahl-i- Hadith		Shia		Total	
	1988	2002	1988	2002	1988	2002	1988	2002	1988	2002	1988	2002
Punjab	43	Nk	500	1176	548	994	118	Nk	21	202	1230	2372+
NWFP	8	Nk	631	382?	32	51	5	Nk	2	13	678	446+
Sindh	6	Nk	208	687	61	487	6	26	10	48	291	1248
B'tan	31	Nk	278	624	34	25	3	Nk	1	15	347	664+
AK	3	Nk	51	36	20	28	2	Nk	Nil	03	76	67+
Islamabad	3	Nk	51	Nk	20	Nk	Nil	Nk	2	7	76	7+
FANA	3	Nk	60	Nk	2	Nk	27	Nk	11	33	103	33+
Girls Madrassas	Nk	40	Nk	Nk	Nk	Nk	Nk	Nk	Nk	Nk	Nk	Nk
Total of Sects	97	500	1779	7000	717	1585	161	376	47	419	2801	9,880

Source: For 1988 GOP 1988. For other figures the sources are given below.

+   The sign of plus means that the number of madrassas is more but cannot be determined.

x   For madrassas in Sindh in 2002, Report by Sindh police quoted in *Dawn* [Karachi] 16 January 2003

@   For Barelvi Madrassas, except those in Sindh, see *Fehrist Madaris-e-Mulhaqa* (Lahore: Tanzeem ul Madris, 1996).

The number of the madrassas given by the Wafaq-ul-Madaris (Shia), Lahore, is 354 which are more than the number which comes from adding the madrassas given in the police report for Sindh.

Nk =Not Known.

Note: Numbers do not add up because the number of madrassas in the provinces is not given for 2002.

ANNEXURE 5

Fact Sheet About Cadet Colleges/Public Schools

Name	Year Estab-lished	Area in Acres	Budget 2002-2003 (Unless otherwise indicated)	* avg. Monthly Tuition fee	Expenditure from fee	Number of Students	@ Cost per year per student	Donation
Aitichison College	1886	196	204,000,000	5,950	80% (163,200,000)	2120	96,226	No Information given by the institution
Cadet College Kohat	1965	144	19,981,217	4,701	44% (8,785,923)	575	34,750	5,819,800 (NWFP Govt)
Cadet College Larkana	1992	362	23,176,006	550	90% (25,817,206)	480	56,617	6,000.00 (Sind Govt)
Cadet College Petaro	1957	425	71,720,000	6,000	80% (57,376,000)	700	102,457	20% (from Sind Govt)
Lawrence College	1860	100	98,886,181	2,000	18.19% (17,987,396)	711	139,080	12,000,000 (Punjab Govt)
Sadiq Public School	1953	150	-	3,500	-	1100	-	1,50,000 from private donors 50,000 per new student 100,000 from Punjab Govt.
Military College Jhelum	1925	167	Salaries from Govt, free rations for cadets + 10,00,000 from GHQ	400 for sons of certain kinds of military personnel and 2000 for others	10% (the other figure is not given by the institution	520	Cannot be calculated	By the GHQ and other donors. Exact figures have not been given by the institution.
Cadet College Hassan Abdal	1954	97	48,223,000	1,350	12.75% (61,53,000)	480	100,465	80,96,000 (Punjab Govt)
Cadet College Mastung	1987	108	36,300,000	2200	15.75% (5,500,000)	360	100,834	Nil

ANNEXURE 6

Yearly Fees in Public Educational Institutions

	Tuition	Others	Total
Schools (up to class 10)	Free in Punjab & NWFP. (Rs. 150 in other areas).	Free or within Rs. 150	Free or within Rs. 150
Colleges Government colleges on the average			**1596**
FA	600	820	1420
F.Sc.	600	892	1492
BA	720	970	1690
B.Sc.	720	1042	1762
Universities	4,400	8,065	12,465

Source and Note: Offices of institutions. The figures for the universities are from Quaid-i-Azam University. Other universities may be cheaper.

ANNEXURE 7

Expenditure on staff in an Urdu-Medium Government School

Post	Expenditure in Rupees (2002-2003)
Principal (x I)	200,000
Vice Principal (x I)	170,000
Headmasters (x 2)	330,000
Deputy Headmasters (x 3)	430,000
Trained Graduate Teachers (x 16)	1,450,000
Trained Under-Graduate Teachers (x 14)	1,220,000
Drawing Master (x I)	55,000
Librarian (x I)	55,000
Total	3,910,000

Source: Office of the Islamia High School, Satellite Town, Rawalpindi.

ANNEXURE 8

Presence of the Military in Armed Forces Universities

University	Board of Governors	CEO	Officers (in May 2003)
NUST	COAS (Chairman); VCAS; VCNS; Minister for Science & Technology; DS; Secretary Science & Technology; Secretary IT; FS; ES; Chairman HEC; PSO of VCAS; Rector (NUST)	Rector (retd. Lt. General)	Most affiliated colleges are military institutions with serving officers.
Bahria	CNS (Chairman); DCNS (T&P); PSOs; Rector, Chairman HEC; ES; FS; STS; VC of any university; DNES; Heads of constituent units; two nominees of industry; two educationists; Dean of Arts and Science.	Rector (retired Vice Admiral)	Registrar, Deputy Registrar, Deputy Director Exams, Assistant Director Exams, Deputy Director Academics.
Air University	CAS (Chairman); VCAS; DCAS (Trg); PSO; Rector, Chairman HEC; ES; STS; VC of any university, three nominees of industry; one judge; three scholars or scientists.	Vice Chancellor (retired Air Marshal)	Director R&D, Project Officer, Deputy Director Finance.
NUML	VCAS (Chairman); Chief Justice, ES; FS; DS; Foreign Secretary, Chairman HEC, D.G. NUML; Senior dean; Registrar; Lt Gen (JSHQ).	Rector (serving brigadier)	Not Known
Foundation University	Chairman: DS MD Fauji Foundation (Lt Gen Retd); Retd Judge of High or Supreme Court; Chairman HEC; ES; VC of any public university; 3 eminent	President	Not known

| academics; 5 nominees of Fauji Foundation; 3 business men | civilian academic |

Key to Abbreviations:	CAS: Chief of Air Staff
	CNS: Chief of Naval Staff
	COAS: Chief of Army Staff
	DCAS(Trg): Deputy Chief of Air Staff (Training)
	DCNS(T&P): Deputy Chief of Naval Staff (Training and Personnel)
	DNES: Director, Naval Education Service
	DS: Defence Secretary
	ES: Secretary of Federal Ministry of Education
	FS: Secretary of the Federal Ministry of Finance
	HEC: Higher Education Commission
	STS: Secretary of the Federal Ministry of Technology and Science
	PSO: Personal Staff Officers (of services chiefs)
	JSHQ: Joint Services Headquarters
	VCAS: Vice Chief of Army Staff
	VCNS: Vice Chief of Naval Staff
	Source:: Offices and brochures of the respective universities.

REFERENCES

Section-1

Primary Sources

Textbook Board Books

Punjab Textbook board. 2002. English: Class-6 Lahore: Punjab Textbook Board. [82,000 copies]
. *2002. English: Class-7* as above [1,80,000 copies]
. *2002. English: Class-8* as above [82,000 copies]
. *1996. English: Class-9* as above [number not indicated]
. *1996. English: Class-10* as above [number not indicated]
. *2002. Social Studies for Class-VII* as above [number not indicated]
. *2002. Social Studies for Class-VIII* as above [number not indicated]
. *2000. Pakistan Studies 9 and 10* as above [number not indicated]
. *2002. Urdu Barae Jamat Sisham* as above [number not indicated]
. *2002. Urdu Barae Jamat Haftam* as above [number not indicated]
. *2002. Urdu Barae Jamat Hashtam* as above [number not indicated]
. *1987. Muraqqa-e-Urdu 9th to 10th* as above [number not indicated]

(b) **Madrassa Books** (*Radd-Texts*)
Qasim, Muhammad. n.d. *Hidayat ul Shi'a* Multan: Taleefat -e-Ashrafiya. [Refutes Shia doctrines].
Usmani, Muhammad Rafi. 1997. *Europe Ke Teen Mu'ashi Nizam*. Karachi: Idara-ul-Mu'arif [Refutes capitalism, socialism and feudalism].
Ludhianwi, Mohammad Yusuf. 1995. *Ikhtilaf-e-Ummat aur Sirat-e-Mustaqim*. Karachi: Maktaba Ludhianwi. [Deobandi point of view about theological controversies].
Nadvi, Syed Abul Hasan Ali n.d. *Muslim Mamalik Mein Islamiat our Maghribiat Ki Kash Makash*. Karachi: Majlis-e-Nashriat-e-Islam. [Historical and philosophical book about the conflict between Islam and Westernization in the Muslim world].
Nomani, Mohammad Manzur. 2002. *Futuhat-e-Nomania: Manazir-e-Ahl-e-Sunnat*. Lahore: Anjuman-e-Irshad ul Muslameen [Discussions between Deobandis and Barelvis written by Deobandis to refute the Barelvis. Very polemical].
Qadri, Arshad ul. 1998. *Zalzala*. Lahore: Shabbir Brothers [A Barelvi text refuting Deobandi doctrines].
Zikria, Mohammad. 1975. *Fitna-e-Maudoodiat*. Lahore: Maktaba ul Qasim [refutes the doctrines of Abul Ala Maudoodi].

Section-2

Secondary Sources

Abdullah, Syed. 1976. *Pakistan Mein Urdu Ka Masla* [Urdu: The Problem of Urdu in Pakistan]. Lahore: Maktaba Khayaban-e-Adab.

Adil, Mukhtar. 1962. *Sindh ki diary* [Urdu: The Diary of Sindh]. J 17 October.

Ahmad, Mumtaz. 2000. 'Continuity and Change in the Traditional System of Islamic Education: The Case of Pakistan'. In Baxter, Craig and Kennedy, Charles H. (eds.) *Pakistan 2000*. Karachi: Oxford University Press.

Ahmad, Saleem. 1968. *Oluh Pakistan men bolin jo maslo.* [Sindhi: The Problem of Languages in West Pakistan]. Khairpur: Privately published.

Ahmad, S. 1987. What we may lose with English. M 7 March.

Ahmed, Khalid. 1999. 'Islamist School Chains and the coming New Order'. *The Friday Times*, 10-16 September.

―――――. 2002. 'The Power of the Ahle Hadith', *The Friday Times* [English weekly from Lahore], 12-18 July.

Ahmed, Rashid. 2003. 'Unpublished Term Paper Submitted as Course Work for M. Phil. in Pakistan Studies', National Institute of Pakistan Studies, Quaid-i-Azam University, Islamabad.

Ahmed, Feroz. 1998. *Ethnicity and Politics in Pakistan*. Karachi: Oxford University Press.

Ahmed, Qeyamuddin. 1994. *The Wahabi Movement in India*. New Delhi: Manohar.

al-Attas, Syed Muhammad al-Naquib. 1979. *Aims and Objectives of Islamic Education*. Kent: Hodder and Stoughton and King Abdul Aziz University, Jeddah.

Amin, Tahir. 1988. *Ethno-National Movements of Pakistan*. Islamabad: Institute of Policy Studies.

Anderson, Benedict. 1983. *Imagined Communities: Reflections on the Origin and Spread of Nationalism*. London: Verso (revised edition) 1991.

Awan, Abdul Ghafoor. 1987. *Private Educational English Medium Institutions in Islamabad and Rawalpindi*. Islamabad: National Language Authority.

Aziz, K.K. 1993. *The Murder of History in Pakistan*. Lahore: Vanguard Press.

Baloch, N.A. 2000. *Education Based on Islamic Values: Imperatives and Implications*. Jamshoro: Pakistan Study Centre, University of Sindh.

Basu, A.N. (ed.) 1952. *Indian Education in Parliamentary Papers*: Part I. Bombay: Asia Publishing House.

Bengali, Kaiser. 1999. *History of Education Policy Making and Planning in Pakistan* Islamabad: Sustainable Development Policy Institute.

Bergen, Peter L. 2001. *Holy War Inc: Inside the Secret World of Osama bin Laden*. New York: Simon & Schuster Inc.

Bhatti, Mukhtar Ahmad. 1987. *Secondary Education in Pakistan: Perspective Planning*. Islamabad: National Education Council.

Census Private. 2001. *Census of Private Educational Institutions 1999-2000*. Islamabad: Federal Bureau of Statistics.

Census. 2001. *1998 Census Report of Pakistan*. Islamabad: Population Census Organization, Statistics Division, Govt. of Pakistan.

Chitnis, Sama and Altbach, Philip G. (ed.) 1993. *Higher Education Reform in India*. New Delhi: Sage Publications.

CII. 1993. *Recommendations on Education 1962-1993.* Islamabad: Council of Islamic Ideology, Government of Pakistan.

Cooley, John K. 1999. *Unholy War: Afghanistan, America and International Terrorism.* London: Pluto Press.

Economic Survey. 1997. *Economic Survey of Pakistan 1996-97.* Islamabad: Govt. of Pakistan, Ministry of Finance.

Edn Comm. 1883. *Report of the Indian Education Commission.* Calcutta: Superintendent of Government Printing.

Edn Ind. 1941. *Education in India in 1938-39.* Delhi: Manager of Publications.

Edn. NWP. 1850. *Memoir on the Statistics of Indigenous Education Within the North Western Provinces of the Bengal Presidency.* R. Thornton (Comp). Calcutta: Printed by J. Thomas, Baptist Mission Press.

EMIS-P. 1998. *Punjab Education Statistics School Census 1997-98.* Lahore: Punjab Education Management Information System, Govt. of Punjab.

EMIS-S. 1998. *Sindh Education Profile: 1993-1996.* Karachi; Education Department, Govt. of Sindh.

Expenditure. 1999. *Details of Demands for Grants and Appropriations 1999-2000 Current Expenditure.* Vols. 1&2. Islamabad: Govt. of Pakistan, Finance Division.

Friedmann, Yohann. 1989. *Prophecy Continuous: Aspects of Ahmadi Religious Thought and Its Medieval Background.* Berkeley: University of California Press.

Fukuyama, Francis. 1992. *The End of History and the Last Man.* New York: The Free Press.

Gilbert, Irene. 1972. 'The Indian Academic Profession: the Origins of a Tradition of Subordination'. *Minerva* 10 (July), 384-411.

Glazer, Nathan and Moynihan, Daniel P. 1975. *Ethnicity: Theory and Experience.* Cambridge, Massachusetts: Harvard University Press.

GoP. 1947. *Proceedings of the Pakistan Educational Conference, 27 November-1st December 1947.* Karachi: Ministry of Interior, Education Division.

————. 1948. *Proceedings of the First Meeting of the Advisory Board of Education for Pakistan.* Karachi: Govt. of Pakistan, Education Division.

————. 1949. *Proceedings of the Second Meetings of the Advisory Board of Education for Pakistan 7th-9th February 1949.* Karachi: Govt. of Pakistan, Education Division.

————. 1950. *Proceedings of the Fourth Meeting of the Advisory Board of Education for Pakistan (29 November- 1st December. 1950)* Karachi: Manager of Publications.

————. 1954. *Proceedings of the Sixth Meeting of the Advisory Board of Education for Pakistan 2nd-5th March, 1954.* Karachi: Manager, Govt. of Pakistan Press.

————. 1959. *Report of the Commission on National Education.* Karachi: Ministry of Education, Government of Pakistan.

————. 1966. *Report of the Commission on Student's Problems and Welfare.* Islamabad: Ministry of Education, Government of Pakistan.

————. 1969. *Proposals for a New Educational Policy.* Islamabad: Ministry of Education and Scientific Research.

————. 1970. *New Education Policy.* Islamabad: Ministry of Education, Government of Pakistan.

————. 1972. *The Education Policy 1972-1980.* Islamabad: Ministry of Education, Government of Pakistan.

————. 1979. *Qaumi Committee Barae Deeni Madaris* [Urdu]. Islamabad: Ministry of Religious Affairs, Government of Pakistan.

_____. 1979b. *National Education Policy and Implementation Programme.* Islamabad: Ministry of Education, Government of Pakistan.

_____. 1988. *Deeni Madaris ki Jame Report* [Urdu]. Islamabad: Islamic Education Research Cell, Ministry of Education, Government of Pakistan.

_____. 1992. *National Education Policy.* Islamabad: Planning Commission, Government of Pakistan.

_____. 1998. *National Education Policy*: 1998-2010. Islamabad: Ministry of Education, Government of Pakistan.

_____. 2002. *Economic Survey of Pakistan: 2001-2002.* Islamabad: Economic Advisory Wing, Finance Division, Govt. of Pakistan.

_____. 2002a. *National Curriculum: Social Studies for Classes VI-VIII.* Islamabad: Government of Pakistan, Ministry of Education.

_____. 2002b. *National Curriculum: History of Pakistan for Classes IX-X.* Islamabad: Govt. of Pakistan, Ministry of Education, March 2002.

_____. 2002c. *Education Sector Reforms: Action Plan 2001-2004.* Islamabad: Government of Pakistan, Ministry of Education.

_____. 2003. *Economic Survey 2002-03.* Islamabad: Govt. of Pakistan, Finance Division, Economic Adviser's Wing.

Haeri, Shahla. 2002. *No Shame for the Sun: Lives of Professional Women.* New York, Syracuse: Syracuse University Press.

Haqqani, Husain. 2002. 'Islam's Medieval Outposts', *Foreign Affairs* (December), 58-64.

Haq, Mahbulul. 1997. *Human Development in South Asia.* Karachi: Oxford University Press.

Hart, James Morgan. 1874. 'German Universities: A Narrative of Personal Experience'. In Graf, Gerald & Warner, Michael (eds.) *The Origins of Literary Studies in America: Documentary Anthology.* New York: Routledge, Chapman & Hall, 1989, pp. 17-24.

Hayes, Louis D. 1987. *The Crisis of Education in Pakistan.* Lahore: Vanguard.

Hoodboy, Pervez. 1991. *Muslims and Science.* Lahore: Vanguard.

_____. 1997. 'Ruins of Khairpur University'. *The News.* 21 May 1997.

_____. (ed.) 1998. *Education and the State: Fifty Years of Pakistan.* Karachi: Oxford University Press.

Hoodbhoy, Pervez and Nayyar, A.H. 1985. 'Rewriting the History of Pakistan'. In Khan, Asghar (ed.). 1985. *Islam, Politics and the State.* London: Zed Press, pp. 164-177.

Hussain, Fayyaz. 1994. 'An Ethnographic Study of Jamia Ashrafia: A religious school at Lahore with Special Emphasis on Socio-practical Relevance of its objective'. M.Sc. Dissertation, Dept. of Anthropology, Quaid-i-Azam University, Islamabad.

Hussain, Mehvish. 2003. 'First Chance', *Herald* (April).

ICG. 2002. *Pakistan: Madrassas, Extremism and the Military.* Islamabad/Brussels: International Advisory Group Asia, Report No. 36, 29 July 2002.

Indireson, P.V. and Nigam, N.C. 1993. 'The Indian institutes of Technology: Excellence in Peril'. In Chitnis & Altbach, 1993: 334-84.

Inyatullah, Sohail and Gidley, Jennifer. (eds.) 2000. *The University in Transformation: Global Perspectives on the Futures of the University.* Westport: Connecticut & London: Bergin & Garvey.

IPS. 1987. *Deeni Madaris ka Nizam-e-Taleem* [Urdu: The System of Education of the Religious Madrassas]. Islamabad: Institute of Policy Studies.

_____. 2002. *Pakistan: Religious Institutions: An Overview.* Islamabad: Institute of Policy Studies.

Jafri, S.H.M. 1979. *The Origins and Early Development of Shia Islam*. Reprint edition. Karachi: Oxford University Press, 2000.

Kazi, Aftab A. 1994. *Ethnicity and Education in Nation Building in Pakistan*. Lahore: Vanguard.

Kazimi, Muhammad Reza. 2003. *Liaquat Ali Khan: His Life and Work*. Karachi: Oxford University Press.

Khalid, Saleem Mansur. 2002. *Deeni Madaris Main Taleem* (Urdu: Education in the Islamic Seminaries). Islamabad: Institute of Policy Studies.

Khan, A. 1967. *Friends Not Masters: A Political Biography*. Karachi: Oxford University Press.

Khan, Shahrukh Rafi. 1991. 'Financing Higher Education in Pakistan'. *Higher Education* 21 (1991), 207-222.

Khan, Shehar Bano. 2003. 'F.C. College: A Pandora's Box', *Dawn* (*Magazine*), 1 June.

Kumar, Krishna. 2001. *Prejudice and Pride: School Histories of the Freedom Struggle in India and Pakistan*. New Delhi: Penguin Books India.

Kraan, J.D. 1984. *Religious Education in Islam with Special Reference to Pakistan: An Introduction and Bibliography*. Rawalpindi: Christian Study Centre.

LAD-WP. *Legislative Assembly Debates: West Pakistan*. [During One Unit, Sindh, Punjab, NWFP, and Balochistan did not have separate legislative assemblies].

Laitin, David D. 1998. *Identity in Formation: The Russian-Speaking Populations in the Near Abroad*. Ithaca and London: Cornell University Press.

Lamb, Alastair. 1997. *Incomplete Partition: The Genesis of the Kashmir Dispute 1947-1948*. Karachi: Oxford University Press.

Liberal Forum. 2003. *Ideas on Democracy, Freedom and Peace in Textbooks: Campaign against hate speech*. Islamabad: Liberal Forum of Pakistan, Future Youth Group.

Mahmoudi, Abdelrashid. 1998. *Taha Husain's Education: From the Azhar to the Sorbonne*. Surrey: Curzon Press.

Makdisi, George. 1981. *The Rise of Colleges: Institutions of Learning in Islam and the West*. Edinburgh: Edinburgh University Press.

Mallet, C.E. 1924. *History of the University of Oxford*. New York: Longmans.

Mandela, Nelson. 1994. *Long Walk to Freedom: The Autobiography of Nelson Mandela*. Boston: Little, Brown and Company.

Mangan, J.A. 1986. *The Games Ethic and Imperialism*. New York: Viking Penguin.

Maudoodi, Abul Ala. 1974. *Talimat* [Urdu: Education]. Lahore: Islamic Publications.

Metcalf, Barbara D. 1982. *Islamic Revival in British India: Deoband, 1860-1900*. Repr. Karachi: Royal Book Company, 1989.

Mirza, Jasmin. 2002. *Between Chaddor and the Market: Female Office Workers in Lahore*. Karachi: Oxford University Press.

Mukherjee (ed.) 1970. *Elites in South Asia*. Cambridge: Cambridge University Press, pp. 172-200.

Myers-Scotton, Carol. 1993. 'Elite Closure as a Powerful Language Strategy: The African Case'. In *International Journal of the Sociology of Language* 103: 149-163.

Nasr, Sayyed Vali Reza. 1996 *Mawdudi and the Making of Islamic Revivalism*. New York: Oxford University Press.

Nayyar, A.H. 1998. 'Madrassa Education: Frozen in Time'. In Hoodbhoy 1998: 213-250.

Nayyar, A.H. and Salim, Ahmed (eds.). 2003. *The Subtle Subversion: The State of Curricula and Textbooks in Pakistan*. Islamabad: Sustainable Development Policy Institute.

Pasha, Hafiz and S. Ashraf Wasti. 1993. 'Social costs of University Closures'. Cyclostyled Conference Paper, Ninth Annual General Meeting, Pakistan Institute of Development Economics, Islamabad.

Pasha, Hafiz. 1995. 'Political Economy of Higher Education: A Study', *Pakistan Economic and Social Review* 33: 102 (Summer/Winter 1995), 19-36.

PEI. 1918. *Progress of Education in India 1912-1917: Seventh Quinquennial Review.* Calcutta: Superintendent of Government Printing.

————. 1939. *Progress of Education in India 1932-37: Eleventh Quinquennial Review.* Delhi: Manager of Publications.

PCST. 2004. *Productive Scientists of Pakistan.* Islamabad: Pakistan Council for Science of Technology.

PIHS. 2002. *Pakistan Integrated Household Survey Round 4: 2001:2002.* Islamabad: Federal Bureau of Statistics, Statistics Division, Government of Pakistan.

Psacharopoulos, George & Woodhall, Maureen. 1985. *Education for Development: An Analysis of Investment Choices.* New York: Oxford University Press for the World Bank.

Quddus, Naseem Jaffer. 1990. *Problems of Education in Pakistan.* Karachi: Royal Book Company.

Quddus, Syed Abdul. 1979. *Education and National Reconstruction of Pakistan.* Lahore: S.I. Gillani.

Rahman, Tariq. 1990. *Pakistani English.* Islamabad: National Institute of Pakistan Studies, Quaid-i-Azam University.

————. 1996. *Language and Politics in Pakistan* Karachi: Oxford University Press.

————. 1998. 'Transforming the Colonial Legacy: The Future of the Pakistani University', *Futures* Vol 30: No. 7, pp. 669-680.

————. 1999. *Language, Education and Culture.* Karachi: Oxford University Press.

————. 2002 *Language, Ideology and Power: Language-Learning among the Muslims of Pakistan and North India.* Karachi: Oxford University Press.

Rashid, Ahmed. 2000. *Taliban: Islam, Oil and the New Great Game in Central Asia.* London: I.B. Tauris.

————. 2002. *Jihad: The Rise of Militant Islam in Central Asia.* Lahore: Vanguard.

Raleigh, T. 1906. *Lord Curzon in India: Being a Selection from His Speeches as Viceroy and Governor General 1998-1905.* London: Macmillan.

Richey, J.A. (ed.) 1922. *Selections from Educational Records Part II: 1840-1859.* Calcutta: Superintendent of Govt. Printing.

Robinson, Francis. 2002. *The Ulema of Farangi Mahal and Islamic Culture in South Asia.* Lahore: Ferozesons.

Rothblatt, Sheldon. 1968. *The Revolution of the Dons: Cambridge and Society in Victorian England.* London: Faber & Faber.

Ross, Murray G. 1976. *The University: The Anatomy of Academie.* New York: McGraw Hill Book Coy.

RPI-F. 1938. *Report on Public Instruction in the North West Frontier Province for the Quinquennium 1932-37.* Peshawar: Manager, Government Stationery and Printing.

————. (1947). *Review on the Annual Report on Public Instruction in the NWFP for 1945-46.* Peshawar: Secretary to the NWFP Government, Home Department.

RPI-S. 1940. *Annual Report on Public Instruction in Sind for 1938-39.* Karachi: The Government Press.

Said, Edward. 1978. *Orientalism.* London and Henley: Routledge & Kegan Paul.

Saigol, Rubina. 1993. *Education: Critical Perspectives*. Lahore: Progressive Publishers.
————. 1995. *Knowledge and Identity: Articulation of Gender in Educational Discourse in Pakistan*. Lahore: ASR Publications.
————. 2000. *Symbolic Violence: Curriculum, Pedagogy and Society*. Lahore: Society for the Advancement of Education.
Sanyal, Usha. 1996. *Devotional Islam and Politics in British India: Ahmad Riza Khan Barelwi and his Movement, 1870-1920*. Delhi: Oxford University Press.
Shils, Edward. 1970. 'The Academic Profession in India'. In Leach, Edmund & Mukherjee, (eds.) 1970. *Elites in South Asia*. Cambridge: Cambridge University Press, pp. 172-200.
Sikand, Yoginder. 2001. 'The Indian State and the Madrasa', *Himal*.
Singer, P.W. 2001. 'Pakistan's Madrassahs: Ensuring a System of Education not Jihad'. Analysis Paper # 14, November 2001. http://www.brookings.edu/views/papers/singer/20020103.htm
Stephens, Joe and Ottaway, David B. 2002. 'From U.S., the ABC's of Jihad in Afghanistan', *The Washington Post,* 23 March 2002, p. 1. Quoted from www//:washingtonpost.com.
Sufi, G.M.D. 1941. *Al-Minhaj: Being the Evolution of Curriculum in the Muslim Educational Institutions of India*. Delhi: Idarah-i-Adabiyat-i-Dilhi. This edition. 1977.
Sullivan, James. 1832. 'Evidence before the Parliamentary Committee on the Affairs of the East India Company'. In Basu, A.N. (ed.) 1952.
Task Force. 2002. *Report of the Task Force on Improvement of Higher Education in Pakistan*. Islamabad: Ministry of Education, Govt. of Pakistan.
Ulich, R. 1965. *Education in Western Cultures*. New York: Harcourt, Brace & World.
UGC. 1987. *Handbook of Universities of Pakistan 1987*. Islamabad: University Grants Commission.
————. 1994. *Handbook of Universities of Pakistan 1994*. As above.
————. 1997. 'Reforms in Affiliation & Examination System in the General Universities of Pakistan'. Cyclostyled Report, UGC. Islamabad, 25 July 1997.
————. 1999. *Colleges of Pakistan 1999*. Islamabad: University Grants Commission.
————. 2001. *Universities of Pakistan*. Islamabad: University Grants Commission.
Veblen, T. 1965. *The Higher Learning in America*. New York: Sentry Press.
Vittachi, Varindra T. 1987. *The Brown Sahib (Revisited)*. Harmondsworth: Penguin Books.
World Bank. 1990. *Higher Education and Scientific Research for Development in Pakistan*, vols. I & II. Confidential Report No. 8231-Pak.
Zachariah, Matthew. 1993. 'Examination Reform in Traditional Universities'. In Chitnis and Altbach, 1993: 155-206.
Zaman, Umme Salma. 1981. *Banners Unfurled: A Critical Analysis of Developments in Education in Pakistan*. Karachi: Royal Book Company.
Zaman, Muhammad Qasim. 1999. 'Religious Education and the Rhetoric of Reform: The Madrassa in British India and Pakistan', *Comparative Studies in Society and History*, Vol. 41, No. 2.
————. 2002. *The Ulama in Contemporary Islam: Custodians of Change*. Princeton: Princeton University Press.
Zaidi, Z.H. (ed.) 1999. *Jinnah Papers: Pakistan at Last (26 July-14 August 1947)*. First Series; Vol. IV. Islamabad: Quaid-i-Azam Papers Project.

Section–3

Interviews

Many *ulema* and most students of *madrassas* did not want their interviews to be recorded by name. Those who allowed their names to be mentioned are listed below:

Arshad, Irshad (Brigadier). 1997. 'Interview of the Principal of Army Burn Hall College (Boys)'. 29 June, Abbottabad.

Hussain, Mohammad. 2002. 'Interview of the Nazim-e-Daftar of Jamiat us Safia', Islamabad, 13 December.

Hasan, Iftikhar (Colonel). 2003. Conversations and telephone interview of Col. Iftikhar Hasan, Director of the NWFP Workers Schools, April and May, Peshawar.

Nabi, Mohammad. 1998. 'Interview of Owner and Head Master of Hira School Matiltan'. 18 June, 9 kilometers from Kalam, Swat.

Naqvi, Iffat (Ms). 1999. 'Interview of Principal, Federal Government Girls Higher Secondary Model School (I/9)', 19 March, Islamabad.

Mitha, Yameema. 2003. Interview of the Owner and Principal of Mazmun-e-Shauq School, F-8/3 Islamabad, 30 October.

Noon, Viqarunnisa. 1994. 'Interview of Lady Noon, President of the Islamabad Chapter of the English Speaking Union', Islamabad, 29 December.

Zafar, Mohammad Iqbal. 2002. 'Interview of the Head of Jamia Rizvia Zia ul Uloom', Satellite Town, Rawalpindi, 26 December.

INDEX